J
910
FARNDON
W9-ARK-797
you should know
about geography
$19.95
PT

GEOGRAPHY

GEOGRAPHY

John Farndon
Consultant: Clive Carpenter

Mason Crest
Publishers

Mason Crest Publishers Inc.
370 Reed Road, Broomall, PA 19008
(866) MCP-BOOK (toll free)
www.masoncrest.com
This edition first published in 2003

Miles Kelly Publishing,
Bardfield Centre, Great Bardfield, Essex, CM7 4SL, U.K.

2 4 6 8 10 9 7 5 3 1

Library of Congress Cataloging-in-Publication data on file at the Library of Congress

ISBN 1-59084-465-3

Editorial Director: Anne Marshall
Editors: Amanda Learmonth, Jenni Rainford
Assistant: Liberty Newton
Americanization: Cindy Leaney
Written and designed by: John Farndon and Angela Koo

Printed in China

CONTENTS

KEY

Asia

The Americas

Europe

Africa and Australasia

People

Places

The Alps

▲ *The pointed summit of the Matterhorn is the third highest peak of the Alps.*

- **The Alps** are Europe's largest mountain range, 653mi (1,050km) long, up to 150mi (250km) wide and covering 81,000 sq mi (210,000 sq km).
- **The highest Alpine peak** is Mont Blanc, 15,771ft (4,807m) on the France–Italy border.
- **Famous peaks** include the Matterhorn and Monte Rosa.

★ STAR FACT ★
The highest village in the Swiss Alps is Juf which lies at a height of 6,975ft (2,126m).

- **The Alps began to form** about 65 million years ago (mya) when the African crustal plate shifted into Europe.
- **The Alps are the source** of many of Europe's major rivers such as the Rhone, Po, and Danube.
- **Warm, dry winds** called föhns blow down leeward slopes, melting snow, and starting avalanches.
- **The high Alpine pastures** are famous for their summer grazing for dairy cows. In winter, the cows come down into the valleys. This is called transhumance.
- **The Alps** are being worn away by human activity. In valleys, cities and factories are growing, while skiing wears away the slopes at the tops of the mountains.
- **The Alps** have Europe's highest vineyards, 4,920ft (1,500m) up.

Thailand and Myanmar

▶ *Many canals thread through Bangkok and provide a way for poor people to bring goods to sell.*

- **Thailand:** Capital: Bangkok. Population: 60.8 million. Currency: baht. Language: Thai.
- **Myanmar:** Capital: Rangoon. Population: 49.4 million. Currency: kyat. Language: Burmese.
- **In 1990** the National League for Democracy (NLD) led by Aung San Suu Kyi won free elections in Myanmar but the army has kept them out of power ever since.
- **Growing opium poppies** to make the painkiller morphine and the drug heroin is one of the few ways the people of north Myanmar can make money.
- **The world's best rubies** come from Mogok in Myanmar.
- **Thailand's capital** is called Bangkok by foreigners but its real name has over 60 syllables. Many locals call it Krung Thep which are the first two syllables.
- **Most people in Thailand** and Myanmar still live in the countryside growing rice to eat.
- **Most people** live on fertile plains and deltas—around the Irrawaddy River in Myanmar and the Chao Phraya in Thailand.
- **Millions** of tourists come to Thailand each year to visit the country's beaches, and the attractions of the city of Bangkok.

Greece

- **Capital:** Athens. Area: 50,949 sq mi (131,957 sq km). Currency: euro. Language: Greek.
- **Physical features:** Highest mountain: Mt. Olympus, 9,570ft (2,917m).
- **Population:** 10.6 million. Population density: 207 sq mi (80 sq km). Life expectancy: men 76.0 years; women 81.3 years.
- **Wealth:** GDP: $130.6 billion. GDP per head: $12,320.
- **Exports:** Clothes, olive oil, petroleum products, fruit.
- **Farming:** Greece is so mountainous that less than a third can be cultivated, but a fifth of all workers work on the land, many raising sheep or growing olives or vines for wine.
- **Greece** is the world's third largest grower of olives after Spain and Italy.
- **Greek salad** includes olives and feta cheese from goats milk. In some small villages, bakers allow villagers to cook their food in their *fuorno* oven.
- **More than 11 million** visitors come to Greece each year—some to see the relics of Ancient Greece, but most to soak up the sun.
- **Athens** is the ancient capital of Greece, dominated by the Acropolis with its famous Parthenon temple ruins. Athens is also a modern city, with pollution caused by traffic.

▼ *Greece is one of the most mountainous countries in Europe.*

World trade

- **International trade** is the buying and selling of goods and services between different countries.
- **International trade** has increased so much people talk of the "globalization" of the world economy. This means that goods are sold around the world.
- **The balance of world trade** is tipped in favor of the world's richest countries and companies.
- **Just 200 huge multinational** companies control much of world trade.
- **Just five countries**, the U.S.A., Germany, Japan, France, and the U.K., control almost half world trade.
- **The 30 richest countries** control 82 percent of world trade.
- **The 49 poorest countries** control just 2 percent of world trade.
- **Some countries** rely mainly on just one export. 95 percent of Nigeria's export earnings come from oil; 75 percent of Botswana's come from diamonds.
- **Some countries** such as the U.S.A. want "free trade"—that is, no restrictions on trade; other less powerful nations want tariffs (taxes on foreign goods) and quotas (agreed quantities) to protect their home industries.
- **The World Trade Organization** was founded in January 1995 to police world trade and to push for free trade.

▼ *This diagram shows the proportions of each type of goods traded around the world.*

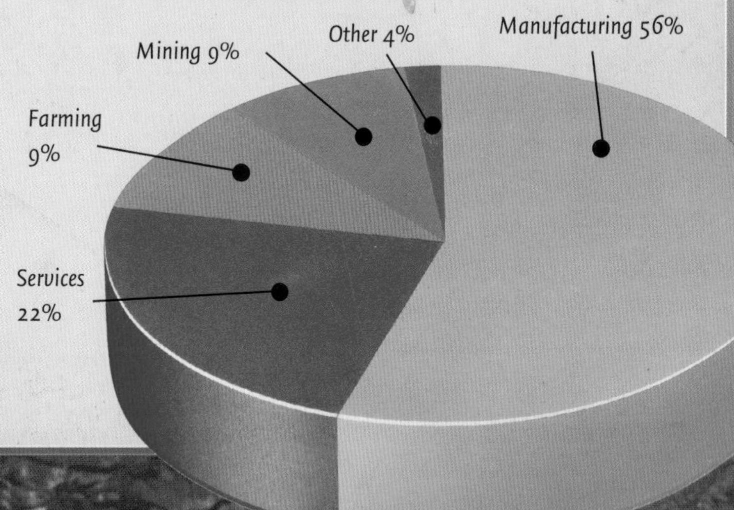

Peoples of northern Asia

- **86 percent of Russians** are descended from a group of people called Slavs who first lived in eastern Europe 5,000 years ago.
- **East Slavs** are the Great Russians (or Russians), the Ukrainians, and the Belarusians(or White Russians).
- **West Slavs** are eastern Europeans such as Czechs, Poles, and Slovaks.

▲ *The Kazakhs or Cossacks were famous for their horseriding skills.*

- **South Slavs** are people such as Croats, Serbs, and Slovenes.
- **Slavs speak** Slavic or Slavonic languages such as Russian, Polish, or Czech.
- **In the old Soviet Union** there were over 100 ethnic groups. 70 percent were Slavs. Many of the rest were Turkic people such as Uzbeks and Kazakhs. Many of these peoples now have their own nations.
- **Slavic** people are mainly Christian; Turkic people are mainly Islamic.
- **Many Turkic peoples** such as the Kazakhs have a nomadic tradition that is fast vanishing.
- **The Mongols** were a people whose empire under the great Khans once spread far south into China and far west across Asia.
- **The Tatars** are 4.6 million Turkic people who now live mainly in the Tatar Republic in the Russian Federation.

Romania and Bulgaria

- **Romania:** Capital: Bucharest. Population: 22.5 million. Currency: leu. Language: Romanian.
- **Bulgaria:** Capital: Sofia. Population: 8.3 million. Currency: Lev. Language: Bulgarian.
- **Romania** gets its name from the Romans who occupied it almost 2,000 years ago.
- **Transylvania** is a beautiful, wooded, mountain area of Romania, once home to the 15th-century tyrant Vlad the Impaler, the original Dracula.
- **Like Bulgaria,** Romania was communist until 1989 when the people overthrew President Ceausescu.
- **Ceausescu's** attempts to develop industry forced people off the lands into towns. Many orphans were left as families broke up.
- **Romania** is a major wine grower.
- **Romania** is home not only to native Romanians but 400,000 Roma (gypsies).
- **The Valley of Roses** is a valley near Kazanluk in Bulgaria full of fields of damask roses.
- **Bulgarian women pick** damask rose blossoms to get the oil to make "attar of roses" used for perfumes.

◀ *Damask rose blossoms in Bulgaria's Valley of Roses are picked early mornings in May and June, before the sun dries out the petals.*

D.R. Congo

- **Capital:** Kinshasa. Area: 905,358 sq mi (2,344,856 sq km.) Currency: Congolese franc. Official language: French.
- **Physical features:** Highest mountain: Mt. Ngaliema, 16,762ft (5,109m). Longest river: Congo, 2,900mi (4,667km).
- **Population:** 51.8 million. Population density: 57 sq mi (22 sq km). Life expectancy: men 49 years; women 52 years.
- **Wealth:** GDP: $5 billion. GDP per head: $110.
- **Exports:** Copper, diamonds, coffee, cobalt, petroleum.
- **D.R. Congo** is called Democratic Republic of Congo to distinguish it from a neighboring country also called Congo, Congo (Brazzaville).
- **Once called the** Belgian Congo D.R. Congo then became the Congolese Republic, then Zaire. Since 1997 it has been the Democratic Republic of Congo
- **D.R. Congo** is one of the world's leading copper producers. There is a vast copper mine in Shaba.
- **D.R. Congo is** the world's leading industrial diamonds producer.
- **The Congo River** is the world's ninth longest river.

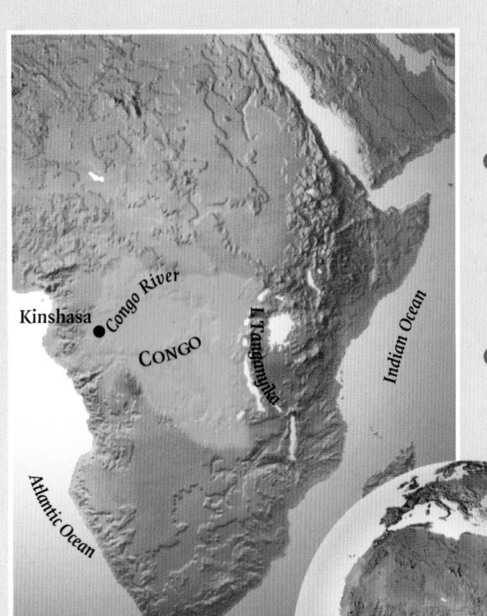

▲ *Congo lies on the Equator. Over a third of it is thick equatorial rain forest.*

Southern U.S.A.

- **The south central states** such as Texas, Oklahoma, and New Mexico produce a lot of oil and gas.
- **Texas** produces more oil than any other state apart from Alaska.
- **One of the world's** largest oil companies was founded on Texan oil.
- **Texas** is known as the Lone Star state.

★ STAR FACT ★
The first integrated circuit was invented in 1958 in Dallas

- **Louisiana** is known as the Sugar state because it grows so much sugar.
- **Oil wealth and aerospace** have attracted high tech industries to Texan cities like Dallas, Houston, and San Antonio.
- **Cotton** is grown on the Mississippi plains, while tobacco is important in the Carolinas and Virginia.
- **In the mid 1800s** the southern states grew 80 percent of the world's cotton, largely using black slave labor.
- **Florida** is famous for Disneyworld, the Cape Canaveral space center and the Everglades, a vast area of steamy tropical swamp infested by alligators.

◀ *Texas's wealth came with the discovery of oil in 1901. Now aerospace and high tech industries are thriving in this sunny state.*

Zimbabwe

▶ *Victoria Falls on the Zambezi is one of the world's biggest waterfalls. Its roar can be heard 20 miles away.*

- **Capital:** Harare. Area: 150,899 sq mi (390,759 sq km). Currency: Zimbabwe dollar. Official language: English.
- **Physical features:** Highest mountain: Mt. Inyangani, 8,513ft (2,592m). Longest river: Zambezi, 1,678mi (2,700km).
- **Population:** 12.4 million. Population density: 72 sq mi (30 sq km). Life expectancy: men 39 years; women 40 years.
- **Wealth:** GDP: $6.3 billion. GDP per head: $520.
- **Exports:** Tobacco, ferrochrome, textiles and clothing, nickel.
- **Zimbabwe** was once the British colony of Rhodesia but was granted independence in 1980.
- **The name Zimbabwe** came from the huge ancient stone palace of Great Zimbabwe.
- **Zimbabwe** is a fertile farming country, growing lots of tobacco, cotton, and other crops. Much of the land still remains in the hands of white farmers, but the government plans to change this situation.
- **Zimbabwe** is the most industrial African nation after South Africa, making steel, cement, cars, textiles, and much more. Harare is the biggest industrial center.
- **98 percent of Zimbabweans** are black. The Shona people are the biggest group, then come the Ndebele (or Matabele).

Chinese food

- **The staple foods** in China are rice and wheat with corn, millet, and sorghum. In the south, the people eat more rice. In the north, they eat more wheat, as bread or noodles.
- **Vegetables** such as cabbage, beans, and bamboo shoots are popular. So too is *tofu* (soya bean curd.)
- **Favorite meats** in China are pork and poultry, but the Chinese also eat a lot of eggs and fish.
- **A Chinese breakfast** may be rice and vegetables or rice porridge and chicken noodle soup or sweet pastries.
- **A Chinese lunch** may include egg rolls or meat or prawn dumplings called *dim sum*.
- **A Chinese main meal** may be stir-fried vegetables with bits of meat or seafood in a stock, with rice or noodles.
- **China has** a long tradition of fine cooking, but styles vary. Cantonese cooking in the south has lots of fish, crabs and shrimps. Huaiyang has steamed dishes. Sichuann is spicy. Beijing cooking in the north is the most sophisticated, famous for its Peking duck .
- **The Chinese** often cook their food by stir-frying (stirring while hot frying) in big round pans called woks. They eat the food from bowls with chopsticks and small china spoons, not with knives and forks.
- **Chinese** drink tea without milk, typically made from jasmine leaves, oolong (green tea), or chrysanthemum.

◀ *A favorite snack in China is fried savory dumplings.*

★ STAR FACT ★
The Chinese were drinking tea at least 4,000 years ago.

Russia

In eastern Siberia, milk is sold in frozen blocks with a wooden handle

▶ *Russia stretches 6,214mi (10,000km)—almost a third of the way around the world—from the open steppes south of Moscow to the chilly pine forests of the Kamchatka in the east.*

Lake Baikal is the world's oldest and deepest lake

Vladivostok is the terminus of the 5,780mi (9438km) Trans–Siberian Railway, the world's longest railroad

- **Capital:** Moscow. Area: 6,592,848 sq mi (17,075,400 sq km). Currency: rouble. Language: Russian.
- **Physical features:** Highest mountain: Mt. Elbrus, 18,510ft (5,642m). Longest river: the Yenisey-Angara 3,443mi (5,540km).
- **Population:** 147.7 million. Population density: 22 sq mi (9/sq km). Life expectancy: men 60.6 years; women 72.8 years.
- **Wealth:** GDP: $330 billion. GDP per head: $2,270. Exports: fuels and lubricants, metals, machinery.
- **Russia** or the Russian Federation is the country created by the Russians after the break up of the Soviet Union in 1991. It includes republics such as Chechnya, Osetiya, Kalmykiya, Tatarstan, Mordoviya, and Bashkortostan. Many of these republics are waiting to be independent.

▼ *The Ural mountains run from north to south forming a natural boundary between Russia and Siberia, Europe and Asia.*

- **Russia is** the biggest country in the world, almost twice as big as the next country, Canada. It stretches from the subtropical south to the Arctic north, where it has the longest Arctic coastline of any country.
- **Russia has huge** mineral resources and is among the world's leading producers of oil, natural gas, coal, asbestos, manganese, silver, tin, and zinc.
- **Russia** has some of the biggest factories in the world around Moscow, producing everything from high tech goods to iron and steel and trucks. Yet in the far north and east, people still live as they have done for many thousands of years, herding reindeer or hunting.
- **After the U.S.S.R. broke up**, Russia and its people were plunged into crisis. Encouraged by western nations, Russian presidents—first Boris Yeltsin, then Vladimir Putin—have tried to establish a free market economy in place of the old communist one.

★ STAR FACT ★

In Yakutsk in Siberia, winter temperatures can plunge to –92.2°F (–69°C) while summers can soar to 102°F (39°C)—more extreme than anywhere else. Oymyakon is the world's coldest town. It once had temperatures of –98°F (–72°C).

New Zealand

◀ New Zealand is made up of two main islands—the almost subtropical North island where most people live and the long, narrow South island with its wide Canterbury Plains, and soaring Southern Alps.

- **Capital:** Wellington. Area: 104,453 sq mi (270,534 sq km). Currency: NZ dollar. Language: English.
- **Physical features:** Highest mountain: Mt. Cook, 12,316ft (3,754m). Longest river: Waikato, 264mi (425km).
- **Population:** 3.8 million. Population density: 35 sq mi (14 sq km). Life expectancy: men 74.3 years; women 79.9 years.
- **Wealth:** GDP: $74.7 billion. GDP per head: $19,660.
- **Exports:** Meat, milk, butter, cheese, wool, fish, fruit.
- **New Zealand** was one of the last places to be inhabited by humans and remains a clean, beautiful land, with rolling farmland, thick forests, and towering mountains.
- **New Zealand** is mainly a farming country, with over 64 percent of the land devoted to crops and pasture for sheep and cattle. Over half of its exports are farm produce.
- **Fast-flowing** rivers provide 61 percent of New Zealand's power through hydroelectric plants. Geothermal energy from hot springs provides some of the rest.
- **The first** inhabitants were the Maoris, who came about AD900 and now form 14.2 percent of the population. The remaining 85.8 percent are mostly descended from British and Irish settlers who came in the 19th and 20th centuries.

★ STAR FACT ★
There are 45 million sheep in New Zealand—12 sheep to every person!

Yellowstone Park

- **Yellowstone** is the oldest and best-known national park in the U.S.A. It was established by Act of Congress on March 1, 1872.
- **It is one of the world's largest** parks covering 3,470 sq mi (8,987 sq km) of spectacular mountains and valleys.
- **It is situated** across Wyoming, Montana, and Idaho.
- **Yellowstone** is famous for its lakes and rivers such Yellowstone Lake and Snake River.
- **Most of Yellowstone** is forested in lodgepole pines, along with other conifers, cottonwoods, and aspens. It also has a wealth of wild flowers.

▼ Yellowstone sits on top of a volcanic hot spot which gives it its famous geysers and hot springs—and may make it the site of the biggest eruption of all time.

- **Yellowstone's** wild animals include bison, elk, bighorn sheep, moose, grizzly bears, and wolves.
- **Yellowstone** has the world's greatest concentration of geothermal features including 10,000 hot springs and 300 geysers, as well as steam vents, mud cauldrons, fumaroles, and paint pots.
- **The most famous geyser** is Old Faithful, which spouts every hour or so. The biggest is the 377ft (115m) Steamboat.
- **One of the biggest** volcanic eruptions ever occured in Yellowstone Park 2 mya. Enough lava poured out to build six Mt. Fujiyamas.
- **There are signs** that Yellowstone may soon erupt as a "supervolcano."

International organizations

◀ *The Red Cross was set up by Swiss Jean Dunant in the 19th century after he witnessed the bloody slaughter at the battle of Solferino in Italy. It now plays a vital role in helping suffering people everywhere.*

- **International organizations** are of three main types: those set up by governments, like the UN; multinationals; and human rights and welfare organizations like the Red Cross and Amnesty International.
- **The United Nations** or UN was formed after World War II to maintain world peace and security. It now has over 190 member nations.
- **UN headquarters** are in New York City. The name was coined by U.S. President Roosevelt in 1941.
- **All UN members** meet in the General Assembly. It has five permanent members (Russia, U.S.A., China, France, and U.K.) and ten chosen every two years.
- **The UN** has agencies responsible for certain areas such as children (UNICEF), food and farming (FAO), health (WHO), science (UNESCO) and nuclear energy (IAEA).
- **Multinationals** or TNCs (transnational corporations) are huge companies that work in many countries.
- **TNCs** like Coca-Cola and Kodak are well known; others like cigarette-makers Philip Morris are less known.
- **Some TNCs** take in more money than most countries. Just 500 TNCs control 70 percent of all the world's trade.
- **90 percent of world** grain is handled by six big U.S. TNCs. Cargill and Continental alone control half the world's grain.
- **Amnesty International** was founded in 1961 to campaign for those imprisoned for religious and political beliefs.

Italy

- **Capital:** Rome. Area: 116,311 sq mi (301,277 sq km). Currency: euro. Language: Italian.
- **Physical features:** Highest mountain: Monte Bianco di Courmayeur, 15,216ft (4,768m). Longest river: Po, 405mi (652km).
- **Population:** 57.3 million. Population density: 445 sq mi (190 sq km). Life expectancy: men 75.4 yrs; women 82.1.
- **Wealth:** GDP: $1,240 billion. GDP per head: $22,650.
- **Exports:** Wine, machinery, cars and trucks, footwear, clothes, olive oil, textiles, mineral products.
- **Italy** is a narrow, mountainous country. The north is cool and moist, with big industrial cities. Tuscany and Umbria have rich farmland and ancient cities famous for their art treasures. The south is hot, dusty, and often poor.
- **Vines and olives** are grown widely and Italy is one of the world's main producers of both wine and olive oil.
- **Italy is one of the biggest** industrial nations. Industry is concentrated in the north in cities like Turin and Milan.

▲ *The ancient city of Venice is set on 117 islands in a lagoon. Instead of streets, there are 177 canals, plied by boats called gondolas.*

Here they make cars, computers, chemicals, and textiles.

- **Italians** like to dress in style and the fashion trade is big business with fashion labels like Armani and Versace.
- **Italy is full of beautiful** historic towns like Florence, Padua and Mantua, many dating from the Renaissance.

Rich and poor

▶▼ Expensive cars and fine foods are often seen as status symbols for the wealthy.

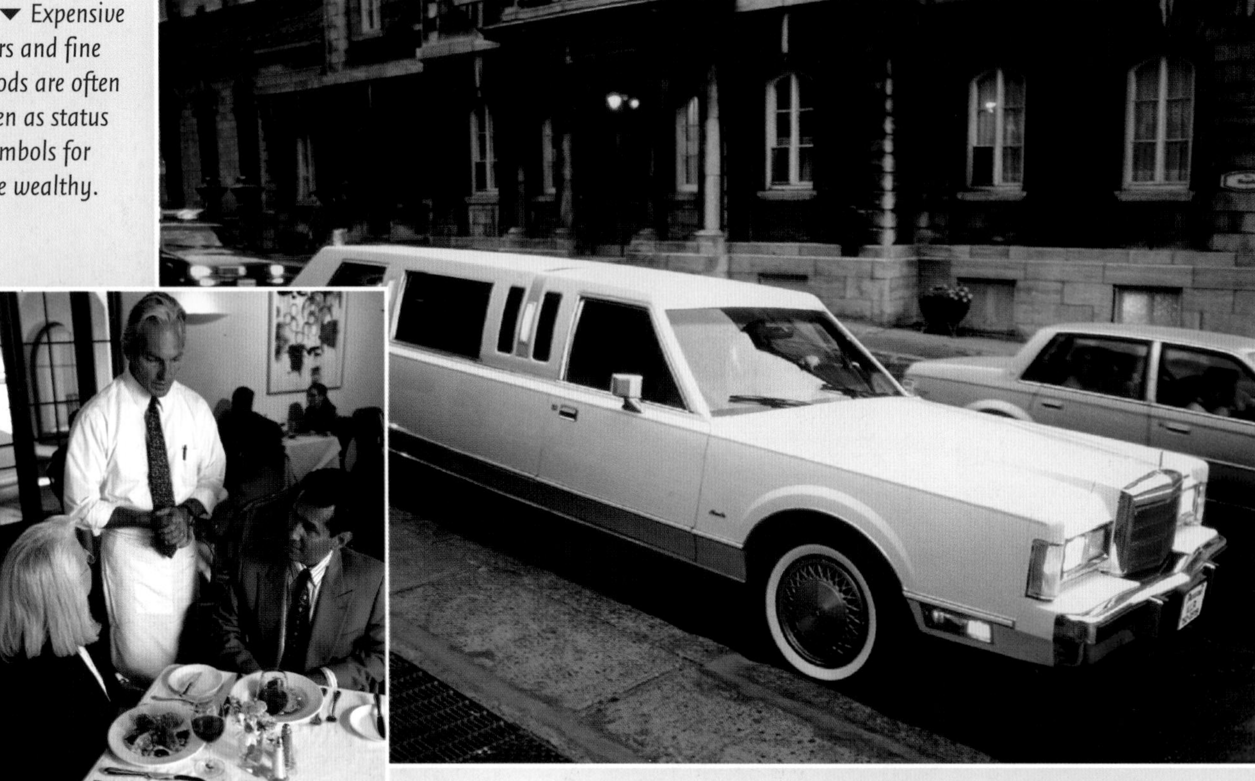

★ STAR FACT ★
About half a billion people are starving or don't get enough to eat.

- **The world's richest country** is the U.S.A., with a GDP of $8,650 billion ($31,330 per head). But Luxembourg has an even higher GDP per head—$45,320.
- **The world's poorest country** by GDP per head is Sierra Leone. Each person has, on average, $130, but many are even poorer.
- **The world's richest countries** with less than a quarter of the world's population take three-quarters of its wealth.
- **Most of the world's rich countries** are in the Northern Hemisphere. Most poor countries are in the South. So people talk of the North–South divide.
- **One billion people** around the world live in "absolute poverty." This means they have no real homes. In cities, they sleep on the street or live in shacks. They rarely have enough to eat or drink.
- **In the 1970s** richer countries encouraged poorer countries like Mexico and Brazil to borrow money to build new dams and industrial works.
- **By 1999** poor countries were paying $12 in debt interest for every $1 rich countries were donating in aid.
- **Famine** has become a common problem in the poorer parts of the world. One reason is that so much farmland is used for growing crops for export—raising the cost of food, and restricting the land available for growing food for local people.
- **250,000** children die a week from a poor diet. 250,000 die a month from diarrhea, because of a lack of clean water.

◀ Since 1960, the divide between North and South has grown wider leaving many in abject poverty.

Israel

- **Capital:** Jerusalem. Area: 8,020 sq mi (20,770 sq km). Currency: new shekel. Languages: Hebrew, Arabic.
- **Physical features:** Highest mountain: Mt. Meron, 3,963ft (1,208m). Longest river: River Jordan 202mi (325km).
- **Population:** 6.1 million. Population density: 774 sq mi (299 sq km). Life expectancy: men 75 years; women 79.9 years.
- **Wealth:** GDP: 107.2 billion. GDP per head: $17,570.
- **Exports:** Diamonds, chemicals and chemical products, fruit and vegetables, machinery.
- **Israel** was founded in 1948 as a home for Jews who have since come here from all over the world.

★ **STAR FACT** ★
Jerusalem is sacred for three major religions: Judaism, Islam, and Christianity.

- **The city of Jericho** may be the oldest in the world, dating back more than 10,000 years.
- **Some people** in rural areas work on kibbutzim—collective farms where work and profits are shared.
- **Israel is famous** for its Jaffa oranges, named after Jaffa, the old name for a town close to Tel Aviv.

Rome

- **Rome** is the capital of Italy, and its biggest city, with a population of almost three million.
- **Rome's Vatican** is the home of the Pope.
- **The Vatican** is the smallest independent country in the world covering just 0.15 sq mi (0.4 sq km).
- **Rome is known** as the Eternal City because of its importance within the Roman Empire.
- **Ancient Rome ruled** much of Europe and the lands around the Mediterranean for hundreds of years as the capital of the Roman Empire.
- **Ancient Rome** was famously built on seven hills: the Aventine, Caelian, Capitoline, Esquiline, Palatine, Quirinal, and Viminal.
- **Rome has** one of the richest collections of art treasures and historic buildings in the world. The Trevi is one of many beautiful fountains.
- **There are many ancient Roman** relics in Rome including the Colosseum arena and the Pantheon.

▲ *St. Peter's Church is located in the Vatican city in Rome.*

- **The Vatican's** Sistine Chapel has a ceiling painted brilliantly by Michelangelo and frescoes (wall paintings) by Botticelli, Ghirlandaio, and Perugino.
- **Rome is** now a major center for film-making, publishing, and tourism.

Peoples of Africa

- **Africa has been** inhabited longer than any other continent. The earliest human fossils were found here.
- **In the north** in countries such as Algeria, Morocco, and Egypt, people are mainly Arabic.
- **The Berber people** were the first people to live in northwest Africa, with a culture dating back to at least 2400BC. Their culture survives in remote villages in the Atlas mountains of Algeria and Morocco.

◀ *Zulus are Bantu-speaking people who live in South Africa. They have a proud warrior tradition.*

- **There are more than 3,000** ethnic groups of black Africans.
- **Over 1,000** different languages are spoken in Africa.
- **Most people** in southern Africa speak English or one of 100 Bantu languages such as Zulu or Swahili.
- **Many people** in rural southern Africa live in round houses.
- **Tuaregs** are camel-herding nomads who live in the Sahara desert, but much of their traditional grazing land has been taken over by permanent farms.
- **South of the Sahara** most people are black Africans.
- **Africa was ruled** by the Europeans as colonies. By the early 20th century the country was divided into nations. Many small groups became dominated by tribes and cultures perhaps hostile to their own.

Turkey and Cyprus

- **Turkey:** Capital: Ankara. Population: 65.7 million. Currency: Turkish lira. Language: Turkish.
- **Cyprus:** Capital: Nicosia. Population: 757,000. Currency: Cyprus pound. Languages: Greek and Turkish.
- **Turkey lies** partly in Europe, partly in Asia. The two continents are separated by a narrow sea called the Bosphorus.

◀ *A hubble-bubble is a special pipe popular in Turkey. Sucking on the long pipe draws the smoke bubbling through water.*

- **Turkey is a republic** with a mix of Islamic and Western traditions.
- **Istanbul** is one of the great historic capital cities. As Byzantium, it was capital of the Byzantine Empire for 1,000 years. Then it was Constantinople, the capital of the great Ottoman Empire for 500 years, until 1923.
- **Street cafés** are popular with Turkish men, who come to drink thick, dark, sweet Turkish coffee, smoke pipes called hubble-bubbles, and play backgammon.
- **An estimated 25 million Kurds** live on the borders of Turkey, Iran, Iraq, and Syria and have no country of their own.
- **31 percent Turkish people** live in the country growing wheat, cotton, tobacco, sugar beet, and tea.
- **Turkey's national motto** is *Yurtta sulh, Cihand sulh* ("Peace at home, peace in the world").
- **Turkish food** is famous for its *shish kebabs*—cubes of meat and vegetables barbecued on a skewer.

Venezuela & neighbors

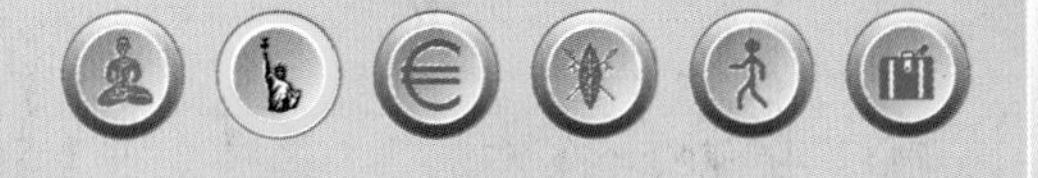

▲ *Venezuela and its neighbors lie along the northern coast of South America, along the edge of the tropical waters of the Caribbean.*

- **Venezuela:** Capital: Caracas. Population: 24.2 million. Currency: bolivar. Language: Spanish.
- **Colombia:** Capital: Bogota. Population: 42.3 million. Currency: Colombian peso. Language: Spanish.
- **Guyana:** Capital: Georgetown. Population: 875,000. Currency: Guyana dollar. Official language: English.
- **Suriname:** Capital: Paramaribo. Population: 452,000. Currency: Suriname guilder. Language: Dutch.
- **French Guiana:** Capital: Cayenne. Population: 114,000. Currency: French franc. Language: French.
- **The discovery of oil** in Venezuela's Lake Maracaibo in 1917 turned it from one of South America's poorest countries to one of its richest.
- **The Venezuelan city** of Merida has the world's highest cable car.
- **The world's highest waterfall** is the Angel Falls in Venezuela, plunging 3,125ft (97m).
- **The Yanomami** are native people who survive in remote forest regions of Venezuela and live by hunting with spears and gathering roots and fruit.
- **Kourou** in French Guiana is the launch site for European spacecraft such as the Ariane.

New York

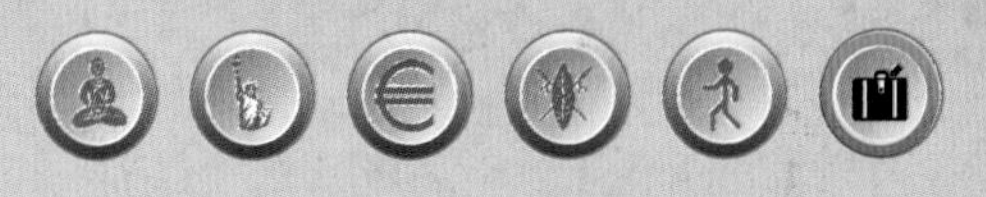

★ STAR FACT ★
New York is the U.S.A.'s largest port and the finance center of the world.

- **New York City** is the largest city in the U.S.A. and one of the largest in the world, with a population of 8 million.
- **Over 21 million people** live in the New York metropolitan area.
- **New York has five** boroughs: Manhattan, Brooklyn, the Bronx, Queens, and Staten Island.
- **Within the five boroughs** are more than 100 neighborhoods, such as Chinatown, Greenwich Village, and Harlem.
- **Manhattan** is the oldest part of the city, and is home to many attractions, including Central Park and Wall Street.
- **The 1,250ft (381m) high** Empire State Building, situated on Fifth Avenue, is one of the world's tallest and most famous buildings.
- **Dutch settler** Peter Minuit bought Manhattan island from Iroquois Indians for trinkets worth $24.
- **New York** began in 1614 with the Dutch settlement of Fort Orange. It was renamed New York in 1664.
- **New York's famous** finance center Wall Street is named after a protective wall built by Dutch colonists in 1653.

▼ *The Statue of Liberty, given to the United States by France in 1884, stands at the entrance to New York harbor.*

Population

- **The world's population** climbed above 6 billion in 1999.
- **Over a quarter** of a million babies are born every day worldwide.
- **World population** is growing at a rate of about 1.22 percent per year.

Asia: 60.7%

Oceania: 0.5%

Africa: 12.7%

Europe: 12.4 %

Antarctica: 0%

North America: 5.2%

South America: 8.5%

◀ *People are not spread evenly around the world. Some continents, like Europe, are densely populated. Antarctica is empty. The size of the figures in this diagram shows the size of the population of each continent. The size of the segment the figure is standing on shows the area of the continent.*

- **Asia has** about 60 percent of the world's population. China has 1.3 billion people and India has 1 billion.
- **At the current rate** world population will hit 7.5 billion by 2020.
- **Between 1950 and 1990**, the world's population doubled from about 2.5 billion to 5 billion, adding 2.5 billion people in 40 years.
- **The 1990s** added a billion people. The next decade will add 800 million.
- **The number of babies** born to each woman varies from 1.11 in Bulgaria to 7.11 in Somalia.
- **Latvia** has 100 women to every 8 men; Qatar has 184 men to every 100 women.
- **In the developed world** people are living longer. In Japan people expect to live 80 years on average. In Mozambique, people only expect to live 36.6 years.

Berlin

- **Berlin** is Germany's capital and largest city, with a population of about 3.5 million.
- **Berlin** was originally capital of Prussia, which expanded to become Germany in the 1800s.
- **The city** was wrecked by Allied bombs in World War II.
- **After the War** Berlin was left inside the new communist East Germany and split into East and West by a high wall.

★ STAR FACT ★
Almost every Berliner has a fragment of the Wall, torn down in 1989.

- **East Berlin** was the capital of East Germany; the West German capital moved to Bonn.
- **In 1989** the East German government collapsed and the Berlin Wall was torn down. East and West Germany were united in 1990 and Berlin was made capital again.
- **The Brandenburg Gate** is a huge stone arch built in 1791. It now marks the boundary between east and west.
- **Kurfurstendamm** is a famous shopping avenue. The Hansa quarter was designed by architects in the 1950s.
- **Since reunification** many spectacular new buildings have been built in Berlin including the refurbished Reichstag designed by Norman Foster.

◀ *When Germany was reunited, the old Reichstag became home of the German parliament again. It has been given a major facelift.*

The U.S.A.

Seattle
Cascade Range
Rocky Mountains
Coast Ranges
Great Basin
San Francisco
CALIFORNIA
Grand Canyon
Los Angeles
Lake Superior
Lake Michigan
Chicago
Detroit
NEW ENGLAND
New York
WASHINGTON D.C.
Appalachian Mountains
Atlanta
Houston
New Orleans
FLORIDA
Miami

The Great Lakes hold a fifth of the world's fresh water

The Pilgrim Fathers of the famous ship the Mayflower landed at Plymouth, Massachusetts in 1620

► *The United States is the richest and most powerful country in the world. Nearly 280 million people live here, and it covers a vast area of North America, from the freezing wastes of Alaska to the hot and steamy Everglades (marshes) of Florida.*

Where it flows into the Gulf of Mexico, North America's longest river, the Mississippi, creates a huge delta

Disney World in Orlando, Florida, is one of the world's biggest theme parks

- **Capital:** Washington D.C. Area: 3,679,459 sq mi (9,529,063 sq km). Currency: U.S. dollar. Language: English.
- **Physical features:** Highest mountain: Mt. McKinley, 20,321ft (6,194m). Longest river: the Mississippi–Missouri-Red Rock, 3,740mi (6,020km).
- **Population:** 281.4 million. Population density: 53 sq mi (29 sq km). Life expectancy: men 73.4 years; women 80.1.
- **Wealth:** GDP: $8,650 billion. GDP per head: $30,725.
- **Exports:** Road vehicles, chemicals, aircraft, generators, machinery, office equipment, scientific instruments.
- **Native Americans lived** in North America for 10,000 years before the Europeans arrived in the 16th century and gradually drove westward, brushing the Native Americans aside. In 1788, English colonists founded the United States of America, now the world's oldest democratic republic, with a famous constitution (set of laws).
- **The U.S.A.** is the world's fourth largest country in area, third largest in population, and has the largest GDP.
- **In the 1950s and 60s** Americans earned more money, ate more food, used more energy, and drove more cars than anyone else in the world.

★ STAR FACT ★

One in two Americans owns a computer—more than any other country in the world.

- **Now the U.S.A.** is the world's prime consumer of energy, oil, copper, lead, zinc, aluminum, corn, coffee, and cocoa. It is also prime producer of aluminum and corn, and one of the top five producers of energy, oil, copper, lead, zinc, wheat, and sugar.

▼ *Through the films made in Hollywood, California, most of the world has become familiar with the American "dream" of success.*

Moscow and St. Petersburg

▲ *St. Petersburg is an elegant city with many beautiful houses and palaces, such as the famous Hermitage museum.*

- **Moscow** is the largest city in the Russian Federation and capital of Russia.
- **Moscow** is Russia's main industrial center, with huge textile and car-making plants, like the Likhachyov works.

> ★ **STAR FACT** ★
> Leningrad was dubbed "Hero City" for its desperate defense against the Nazis from 1941–44.

- **Moscow's biggest shop** is Detsky Mir (Children's World).
- **Moscow's historic center** is Red Square and the Kremlin, the walled city-within-a-city.
- **In the past** Moscow had wooden buildings and was often burnt down, most famously by Napoleon's troops in 1812.
- **Moscow is snow-covered** from November to April each year, but snow-plows keep all the main roads clear.
- **St. Petersburg** is Russia's second largest city.
- **St. Petersburg** was founded in 1703 by Tsar Peter the Great to be his capital instead of Moscow.
- **After the 1917 Russian Revolution**, communists called Petersburg (then called Petrograd) Leningrad and made Moscow capital. St. Petersburg regained its name in 1991.

India

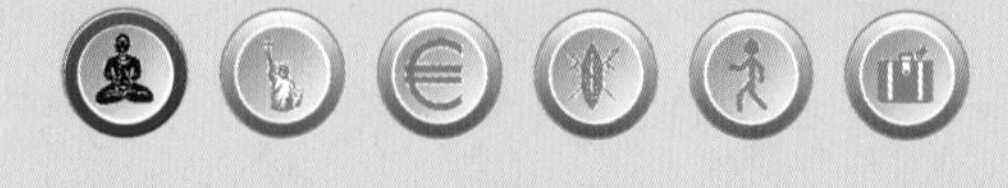

- **Capital:** New Delhi. Area: 1,269,219 sq mi (3,287,263 sq km). Currency: Indian rupee. Languages: Hindi and English.
- **Physical features:** Highest mountain: Kanchenjunga, 28,209ft (8,598m). Longest river: Ganges, 1,560mi (2,510km).

▼ *Hindu women in India traditionally wear beautifully colored wraps or saris made of fine cloth such as silk.*

- **Population:** 1 billion. Population density: 803 sq mi (310 sq km). Life expectancy: men 59.6 years; women 61.29 years.
- **Wealth:** GDP: $473.4 billion. GDP per head: $464.
- **Exports:** Gems, jewelry, clothes, cotton, rice, textiles, tea, engineering goods.
- **India has heavy** monsoon rains for six months of the year and dry weather for the rest.
- **India is the world's** largest democracy.
- **Two-thirds** of India's population grow their own food, mainly rice and wheat.
- **India's wheat production** has doubled since the "Green Revolution" of the 1960s.
- **India is the world's** 12th biggest industrial nation. Heavy industry is growing in importance.

Brazil

- **Capital:** Brasilia. Area: 3,300,411 sq mi (8,547,404 sq km). Currency: real. Language: Portuguese.
- **Physical features:** Highest mountain: Neblina, 9,888ft (3,014m). Longest river: the Amazon, 4,007mi (6,448km).
- **Population:** 169.2 million. Population density: 49 sq mi (19 sq km). Life expectancy: men 63.7 years; women 71.7 years.
- **Wealth:** GDP: $990 billion. GDP per head: $5,845.
- **Exports:** Iron ore, coffee, timber, sugar, transportation equipment.
- **Brazil has the biggest** national debt of any country in the world—not far short of $200 billion.

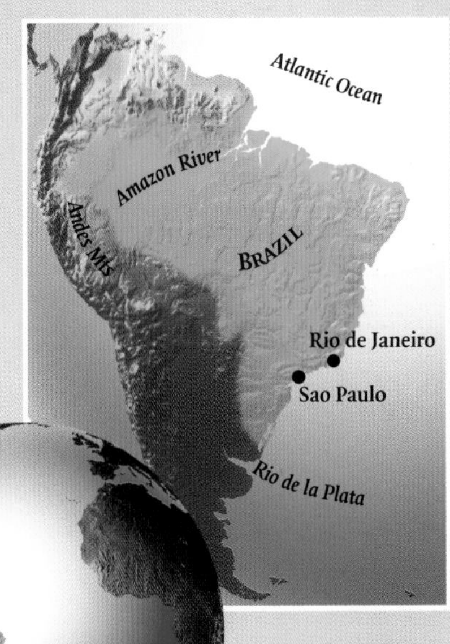

◀ *Brazil is the world's fifth largest country, but most people live on the eastern edge. Much of the central area is cerrado (grass wilderness) or thick Amazon rain forest.*

- **Brazil** is the world's biggest coffee grower. Soya, sugarcane, cotton, oranges, bananas, and cocoa are also major crops.
- **The city of São Paulo** has grown faster than any other big city in the world. Now 17.8 million people live there. Housing shortages in big cities mean 25 million Brazilians live in shanty towns called *favelas*.
- **Brazilians are soccer-crazy** and have won the World Cup more times than any other country.
- **The Amazon basin** contains the world's largest area of virgin rain forest—but an area almost the size of Ireland is being cleared each year for short-term cattle ranching.

North European food

- **Fish and bread** play a major role in the traditional Scandinavian diet.
- **Gravadlax** is a Swedish form of smoked salmon, usually served with pepper, dill, and mustard sauce.
- **Smörgåsbord** is a Swedish speciality. It is a huge spread of bread and cold foods, including fish such as herring and salmon, and also cheeses.
- **Smörgåsbord** gets its name from the Swedish *smörgås*, meaning bread and *bord*, meaning table.
- **Every region in Germany** has its own range of foods, but things like *wurst* (sausages), pretzels, and *sauerkraut* (pickled cabbage) are widely popular.
- **The German national drink** is beer, and every October a huge beer festival is held in Munich.
- **England is well known** for its hearty stews and winter roasts, especially roast beef. But the most popular food for those eating out is Indian.
- **An English speciality** is fish (deep fried in batter) and chips (fried slices of potato.)
- **Vienna** in Austria is renowned for its coffee houses where the Viennese sit and eat *Kaffee und Kuchen* (coffee and cakes).
- **Poland is famous** for its rye bread and thick beet soup.

▼ *The seas around Northern Europe were once teeming with fish. Fish still plays a major role in the diet of people here.*

Japan

- **Capital:** Tokyo. Area: 145,894 sq mi (377,835 sq km). Currency: yen. Language: Japanese.
- **Physical features:** Highest mountain: Mt. Fujiyama, 12,388ft (3,776m). Longest river: the Shinano-gawa, 228mi (367km).
- **Population:** 127 million. Population density: 873 sq mi (337 sq km). Life expectancy: Men 77.6 years; women 84.2 years.
- **Wealth:** GDP: $4,555.1 billion. GDP per head: $35,830.
- **Exports:** Electronic goods, steel, cars, ships, chemicals, textiles, machinery.
- **Japan** is very mountainous, so the big cities where nine out of ten people live are crowded into the coastal plains. 40 million people are crammed into Tokyo and its suburbs alone, making it the biggest urban center in the world. Tokyo has tall skyscrapers to make the most of the limited space available.
- **Japan** is famous for its electronic goods—including walkmans and games consoles. It also makes huge amounts of steel, half the world's ships, and more cars than any other country.

The Seikan Tunnel links Hokkaido to Honshu under the stormy Tsugaru Straits

The Hida, Japan's highest mountains, are also known as the Japanese Alps

◀ Japan is made up of four large islands: Hokkaido, Honshu, Shikoku, and Kyushu: and nearly 4,000 smaller ones, stretching over almost 1,490mi (2,400km) of the western Pacific Ocean. 75 percent of Japanese people live on Honshu, the largest island. But the most densely populated is Kyushu. After some gigantic engineering projects in the late 20th century, Kyushu, Honshu, Shikoku, and other islands are now all linked by bridges and tunnels. The massive Seto Ohashi bridge links several islands. The bridge from Honshu to Shikoku at Akashi-Kaikyo has the world's longest single span: 1.24mi (2km). Hokkaido and Honshu are linked by the Seikan tunnel, the world's longest undersea tunnel, 33.5mi (53.8km) long.

- **All but 14 percent** of the land is too steep for farming, but millions of little square rice fields are packed on to the coastal plains and hillside terraces.
- **Most Japanese live** a very modern way of life. But traditions still survive and there are many ancient Buddhist and Shinto shrines.

★ **STAR FACT** ★

Japan has one of the world's largest fishing fleets which hauls in over 5 million tons of fish a year.

▼ The beautiful, snow-capped Mt. Fujiyama is the most famous of Japan's 1,500 volcanoes and is sacred to the Shinto religion.

Australian landmarks

- **Australia's most famous landmark** is Uluru or Ayers Rock, the biggest monolith (single block of stone) in the world, 1,141ft (348m) high and 5.6mi (9km) around.
- **Uluru** is the tip of a huge bed of coarse sand laid down in an inland sea some 600 mya.
- **Lake Eyre** is Australia's lowest point, 49ft (15m) below sea level. It is also Australia's biggest lake by far, but it is normally dry and fills only once every 50 years or so.
- **Nullarbor plain** is a vast, dry plain in southern Australia. Its name comes from the Latin *nulla arbor* ("no tree").
- **Shark Bay** is famous for its sharks and dolphins.
- **Shark Bay** is also famous for its stromatolites, the world's oldest fossils, dating back 3.5 billion years. These are pizza-like mats made by colonies of blue-green algae.

★ STAR FACT ★
The Great Barrier Reef is the world's largest structure made by living things.

▲ *Uluru is sacred to the Aboriginals. On its surface and in its caves are paintings made long ago by Aboriginal artists.*

- **The Murray–Darling River** is Australia's longest river, 1,702mi (2,739km) long.
- **The Great Barrier Reef** is a coral reef off the coast of Queensland in northwest Australia.
- **The Great Barrier Reef** is the world's biggest coral reef, over 1,242mi (2,000km) long.

Ukraine and Belarus

- **Ukraine:** Capital: Kiev. Population: 50.8 million. Currency: hryvnya. Language: Ukrainian.
- **Belarus:** Capital: Minsk. Population: 10 million. Currency: Belarusian rouble. Language: Belarusian.
- **Ukraine** is Europe's largest country (except for Russia), covering over 231,661 sq mi (603,700 sq km).
- **Ukraine** is famous for its vast plains or *steppes*. The fertile black soils have made it "the breadbasket of Europe," growing huge amounts of wheat and barley.
- **During the Soviet era** Soviet policies forced Ukrainians to speak Russian and adopt Russian culture, but the Ukrainian identity has been found again since they gained independence in 1991.

▶ *Ukraine and Belarus are flat countries that form the western margin of Russia, north of the Black Sea.*

- **In the Soviet era** over a quarter of Ukraine's industrial output was arms. Now Ukraine is trying to use these factories to make other products.
- **In 1986** a terrible accident occurred at the Chernobyl nuclear power plant north of Kiev. A reactor exploded spreading radioactivity over a wide area.
- **Nuclear energy** still provides 44 percent of Ukraine's power, but many Ukrainians are firmly against it.
- **Belarus** (known as Byelorussia under the U.S.S.R.) is a flat country, covered in many places by thick forests and marshes. The Pripet Marshes are the largest in Europe covering 10,425 sq mi (27,000 sq km).
- **Belarus** is known for making heavy-duty trucks, tractors, and bicycles among other things. The forests provide products such as furniture, matches, and paper.

Peoples of Australia

- **The Aborigines** make up 1.8 percent of Australia's population today, but they were the first inhabitants.
- **The word aborigine** comes from the Latin *ab origine*, which means "from the start."
- **Aborigine cave paintings** and tools have been found in Australia dating back to at least 45,000 years ago.
- **Aborigines** prefer to be called Kooris.
- **British and Irish people** began to settle in Australia about 200 years ago. They now form the majority of the population, along with other white Europeans.
- **Many of the earliest** settlers in Australia were convicts, transported from Britain.

◀ *The Kooris or Aborigines of Australia spread right across the Pacific many thousands of years ago and were probably the first inhabitants of America as well.*

- **Many Australians** have ancestral roots in the British Isles.
- **British and Irish settlers** drove the Aborigines from their land and most now live in cities.
- **After hard campaigning** some Aboriginal sacred sites are being returned to them, with their original names. Ayers Rock is now known as Uluru. A famous trial in 1992 returned to Aborigine Eddy Mabo land on Murray Island first occupied by his ancestors before the Europeans arrived.
- **Many recent immigrants** to Australia are from Southeast Asia, Serbia, Croatia, and Greece.

Kazakhstan & neighbors

- **Kazakhstan:** Capital: Astana. Population: 16.93 million. Currency: tenge. Language: Kazakh.
- **Uzbekistan:** Capital: Tashkent. Population: 25 million. Currency: som. Language: Uzbek.
- **Turkmenistan:** Capital: Ashkabat. Population: 4.5 million. Currency: manat. Language: Turkmen.
- **Some of the people** in this part of the world are still nomads, moving from place to place in search of new pastures for their herds.
- **Uzbekistan** has become wealthy from natural gas and also from cotton, which they call "white gold."
- **The Baykonur Cosmodrome** in Kazakhstan is where the Russians launch most of their spacecraft.
- **The Soviet Union** forced nomads in Kalmykia by the Caspian Sea to boost sheep production beyond what the fragile steppe grass could handle. This created 1.4 million acres (0.6 million hectares) of desert.
- **The Aral Sea** on the Kazakh-Uzbek border was once the world's fourth largest lake. But irrigating farmland has cut the supply of water from the Amu Darya River and the Aral Sea is now shrinking rapidly.
- **The Caspian Sea** once had the sturgeon fish giving the most highly prized beluga caviar, but pollution has decimated the fish population.

★ STAR FACT ★
Kazakhstan has huge iron and coal reserves and the world's largest chrome mine.

◀ *The break-up of the Soviet Union left the countries around the Caspian Sea a legacy of some of the world's worst pollution. But they have a wealth of minerals and a venerable history.*

East Africa

▲ *Tanzania is famous for safaris in the Serengeti park where lions, elephants, giraffes, and many other animals are seen.*

- **Tanzania:** Legislative capital: Dodoma. Population: 33.69 million. Currency: shilling. Languages: English and Swahili.
- **Rwanda:** Capital: Kigali. Population: 7.7 million. Currency: franc. Languages: French and Kinyarwanda.
- **Burundi:** Capital: Bujumbura. Population: 6.97 million. Currency: franc. Languages: French and Kirundi.
- **Uganda:** Capital: Kampala. Population: 22.21 million. Currency: shilling. Languages: Swahili, English.
- **Malawi:** Capital: Lilongwe. Population: 10.9 million. Currency: kwacha. Languages: Chewa and English.
- **A fifth of Malawi** is taken up by Lake Nyasa, one of the world's largest, deepest lakes.
- **The countries** of East Africa are the least urbanized in the world with 9 out of 10 living in the countryside.
- **In 1993 and 1994** Rwanda and Burundi were ravaged by one of the worst genocides in African history as tribal war flared between the Tutsi and Hutu peoples.
- **Lake Victoria** on the Tanzania and Uganda border is one of the world's largest lakes.
- **One of Tanzania's** main crops is sisal, a kind of palm.

The Gran Chaco

- **The Gran Chaco** is a vast area of tropical grassland in Argentina, Paraguay, and Bolivia.
- **It covers** an area of over 278,013 sq mi (720,002 sq km), an area as large as northwest Europe.
- **It is home** to scattered native Indian groups such as the Guaycurú, Lengua, Mataco, Zamuco, and Tupi-Guarani people.
- **The word Chaco** comes from the Quechua Indian word for "Hunting Land" because it is rich in wildlife. *Gran* is Spanish for "big."
- **The major activities** on the Chaco are cattle grazing and cotton growing.
- **In the east** huge factories have been built to process tannin from the trees for leather production.

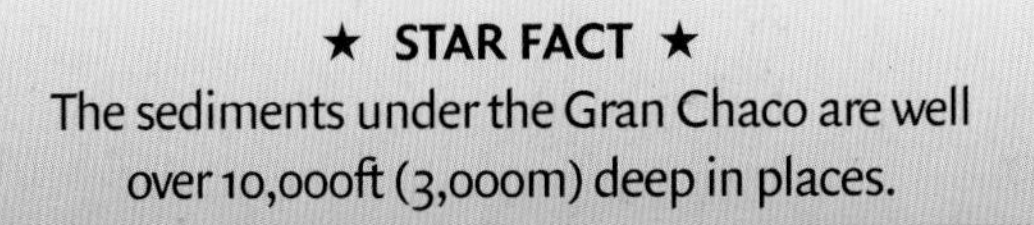

★ STAR FACT ★

The sediments under the Gran Chaco are well over 10,000ft (3,000m) deep in places.

- **In places** grass can grow up to 10ft (3m) tall, higher than a rider on horseback.
- **The Chaco** is home to many wild animals, including pumas, tapir, rheas, and giant armadillos.
- **The Chaco** is the last refuge of the South American maned or red wolf.

▶ *The jaguar is the Chaco's biggest hunting animal, and the biggest cat in the Americas. Yet unlike other big cats, it never roars. It just makes a strange cry rather like a loud sneeze.*

Poland and neighbors

▲ *Poland and its neighbors cluster around the Baltic Sea.*

- **Poland:** Capital: Warsaw. Population: 38.7 million. Currency: zloty. Language: Polish.
- **Lithuania:** Capital: Vilnius. Population: 3.7 million. Currency: litas. Language: Lithuanian.
- **Latvia:** Capital: Riga. Population: 2.4 million. Currency: lats. Language: Latvian.
- **Estonia:** Capital: Tallinn. Population: 1.42 million. Currency: kroon. Language: Estonian.
- **Poland** was led away from communism by trade union leader Lech Walesa, who became the first president democratically elected of Poland for 72 years.
- **The name Poland** comes from the Slavic word *polane* which means plain, as much of Poland is flat plains.
- **The shipyards at Gdansk** on the Baltic make Poland the world's fifth largest builder of merchant ships.
- **Krakow** has many historic buildings but the nearby Nowa Huta steelworks make it very polluted.
- **The traditional way of life** in Latvia, Lithuania, and Estonia suffered badly in the Soviet era. They are now rebuilding their identity.
- **Latvian** is one of the oldest European languages, related to the ancient Indian language Sanskrit.

West Coast U.S.A.

- **The western U.S.A.** is mountainous, with peaks in the Rockies, Cascades, and Sierra Nevada soaring over 13,000ft (4,000m).
- **Seattle** is the home of computer software giant Microsoft, and Boeing, the world's biggest aircraft maker.
- **Seattle** is the home of the Starbucks café chain—made famous by the TV series *Frasier*.

◀ *Sunset Boulevard in L.A. is a 19mi (32km) long road. Its Sunset Strip section is popular with film stars.*

- **Los Angeles** (L.A.) sprawls over a larger area than any other city in the world and has endless miles of freeways.
- **Film-makers** came to the L.A. suburb of Hollywood in 1908 because of California's sunshine. It has been the world's greatest film-making center ever since.
- **The San Andreas fault** is the boundary between two huge continental plates. As it moves it gives west coast cities earthquakes.The worst may be yet to come.
- **San Francisco's** Golden Gate is named after the 1849 rush when prospectors came in thousands to look for gold.
- **California is** known as the "Sunshine State."
- **California's** San Joaquin valley is one of the world's major wine-growing regions.

★ **STAR FACT** ★

Silicon Valley near San Francisco has the world's greatest concentration of electronics firms.

World religions

- **Christianity** is the world's largest religion, with 1.9 billion followers worldwide. Christians believe in a savior, Jesus Christ, a Jew who lived in Palestine 2,000 years ago. Christ, they believe, was the Son of God. When crucified to death (nailed to a wooden cross), he rose from the dead to join God in heaven.
- **Islam** is the world's second largest religion with 1.3 billion believers. It was founded in Arabia in the 7th century by Muhammed, who Muslims believe was the last, greatest prophet sent by *Allah* (Arabic for God). The word *Islam* means "act of resignation" and Muslims believe they must obey God totally and live by the holy book *The Qur'an*.
- **Hinduism** is almost 4,000 years old. Hindus worship many gods, but all believe in *dharma*, the right way to live. Like Buddhists, Hindus believe we all have past lives. By following the *dharma*, we may reach the perfect state of *Moksha* and so need never be born again.
- **Christianity** is split into three branches: Catholics whose leader is the Pope in Rome; Protestants; and the Eastern Orthodox church. Islam is split into Sunnis and Shi'ites. Shi'ites are the majority in Iraq and Iran.
- **Buddhism** is the religion of 350 million Asians. It is based on the teachings of Prince Siddhartha Gautama, the Buddha, who lived in northeast India 563–483BC.
- **Judaism** is the religion of Jews. They were the first to believe in a single god, who they called *Yahweh*, over 4,000 years ago. There are over 11 million Jews living outside Israel and 4.4 million living in Israel.
- **Most of the world's** major religions, except for Hinduism, are monotheistic—that is, they believe in just one God.
- **Three million Muslims** visit their holy city of Mecca in Saudi Arabia every year on pilgrimage.
- **Jains** of India will not take any form of life. They eat neither meat nor fish, nor, usually, eggs. Jain priests often sweep paths in front of them as they go to avoid stepping on insects.

★ STAR FACT ★

The Hindu holy text, the *Bhagaavadgita*, contains almost 100,000 couplets. It is 7 times the length of the *Iliad* and *Odyssey* combined.

▶ *Each major religion except for Christianity is concentrated in one part of the world. Islam, for instance, is practiced mainly in western Asia, the Middle East and North Africa. Hinduism is the major religion in India. Buddhism is practiced widely in Southeast Asia, especially China, Tibet, Thailand, and Cambodia. Christianity is the exception. Most Christians live in Europe, Australia, and the Americas, but the religion was spread around the world by European colonists and missionaries.*

Christianity
Islam
Buddhism
Hinduism
Local beliefs
Largely uninhabited

Peoples of the Middle East

- **People have farmed** in the Middle East longer than anywhere else in the world.
- **The Middle East** was the site of the first cities and ancient civilizations such as those of Sumer and Babylon.
- **Most people** in the Middle East are Arabs.
- **Arabic is spoken** in all Middle East countries except for Iran where Farsi (Persian) is spoken, Turkey where most speak Turkish, and Israel where most speak Hebrew.
- **Most people** in the Middle East are Muslims, but Lebanon has many Christians and Israel is mostly Jewish.
- **Many of the Arab** countries of the Middle East—except Israel—are dominated by Islamic traditions.

▲ *Many people in the Middle East wear traditional Arab head coverings.*

- **Islamic countries** of the Middle East are often ruled by kings and emirs, sultans, and sheikhs who have absolute power. Yemen, Turkey, and Israel are all republics. Iraq is a republic but it is ruled by President Saddam Hussein with absolute power.
- **The Jews of Israel** are locked in a conflict with the Arab people, the roots of which which date back to the 1920s.
- **The people of the United Arab Emirates** (U.A.E.) are among the richest in the world, with a yearly income of over $25,000 each.
- **The people of Yemen** are among the poorest in the world, with a yearly income of just $325 each.

Central America

- **Central American countries** are: Mexico, Guatemala, Belize, Honduras, El Salvador, Nicaragua, Costa Rica, and Panama.
- **Mexico:** Capital: Mexico City. Population: 97 million. Currency: peso. Language: Spanish.
- **Mexico City** is the world's second largest city after Tokyo, with a population of 18.4 million.

▼ *The Panama Canal cuts right across Central America to link the Atlantic and Pacific Oceans and save ships huge journeys.*

- **Most Central American** countries were torn apart by revolution and civil war in the 1900s.
- **Mexico owes** in foreign debt almost $167 billion and pays over $37 billion a year back to other countries.
- **Much land** is used for "cash crops" (crops, like coffee, that can be sold abroad for cash) rather than for food.
- **Many Central Americans** work the land, growing food for themselves or laboring on plantations.
- **Maize** (corn) has been grown in Mexico for 7,000 years to make foods such as tortillas (cornflour pancakes).
- **Bananas** are the most important export in Central American countries, forming a third of Honduras's entire exports. While bananas are grown on lowlands, coffee beans are important exports for highland regions, especially in Nicaragua, Guatemala, Costa Rica, and El Salvador.
- **Most of Mexico's people** are *mestizos*, descendants of both Spanish settlers and American Indians.

Georgia & its neighbors

◀ *Georgia, Armenia, and, Azerbaijan lie in a band between the Black Sea and the Caspian Sea. Georgia and Armenia are mountainous. Azerbaijan is quite flat.*

- **Georgia:** Capital: Tbilisi. Population: 5.42 million. Currency: lari. Language: Georgian.
- **Armenia:** Capital: Yerevan. Population: 3.66 million. Currency: dram. Language: Armenian.
- **Azerbaijan:** Capital: Baku. Population: 8 million. Currency: manat. Language: Azeri.
- **Georgia, Azerbaijan, and Armenia** were once part of the Imperial Russia.
- **In Georgia more people** live to be 100 years old than anywhere else in the world, except Japan.
- **Georgia's capital Tbilisi** is said to be one of the world's oldest cities.
- **The oil** under the Caspian Sea off Azerbaijan once helped the Soviet Union produce half the world's oil. Villages on floating platforms house oilworkers.
- **New oil strikes** suggest there is 200 billion barrels of oil under the Caspian Sea—as much as Iran and Iraq combined.
- **Oil has made** some people around the Caspian Sea rich, while others have remained desperately poor.
- **A pipeline** from Kazakhstan's huge Tengiz field to Russia's Black Sea port of Novorossiysk has recently been opened.

South Africa

◀ *Nelson Mandela was the hero of the struggle against apartheid in South Africa. In 1994 he became the country's first president elected by all the people.*

- **Capitals:** Pretoria and Cape Town. Area: 470,724 sq mi (1,219,080 sq km). Currency: rand. Languages: 11 official languages including Zulu, Xhosa, English, and Afrikaans.
- **Physical features:** Highest mountain: Injasuti, 11,181ft (3,408m). Longest river: the Orange, 1,350mi (2,173km).
- **Population:** 43.7 million. Population density: 93 sq mi (36 sq km). Life expectancy: men 47.3 years; women 49.7.

★ STAR FACT ★
In the 1900s, almost half the world's gold came from South Africa.

- **Wealth:** GDP: $150.3 billion. GDP per head: $3,440.
- **Exports:** Gold, diamonds, pearls, metals, metal products, machinery, citrus fruit, wine.
- **Until 1991** people of different races in South Africa were separated by law—called apartheid.
- **Apartheid** meant many black people were forced to live in specially built townships such as Soweto. Townships are far from cities and workplaces, so workers must commute for hours each day on crowded buses.
- **South Africa** has two capital cities. The administration is in Pretoria and parliament is in Cape Town.
- **The Kruger National Park** supports the greatest variety of wildlife species on the African continent.

Germany

▲ Neuschwanstein, built for "Mad" King Ludwig II of Bavaria in the 1870s, is the most famous of the many castles in Bavaria and Germany's Rhineland.

▶ The flatter northern part of Germany is a mixture of heath, marsh, and rich farmland, where cereals such as rye are widely grown. The south is mountainous, with powerful rivers flowing through deep, wooded valleys.

Hamburg is Germany's biggest port

Germany's northwest is known as Saxony

When trees began to die from acid rain in the famous Black Forest, many Germans became committed to the Green cause. The country now has strong environment protection laws

Germany's longest river, the Rhine, rises in the high Alpine mountains in the country's south

- **Capital:** Berlin. Area: 138,224 sq mi (357,973 sq km). Currency: euro. Language: German.
- **Physical features:** Highest mountain: Zugspitze, 9,721ft (2,963m). Longest river: the Danube, 1,776mi (2,859km).
- **Population:** 82.69 million. Population density: 589 sq mi (231 sq km). Life expectancy: men 74 years; women 80.3 years.
- **Wealth:** GDP: $2,257 billion. GDP per head: $27,300.
- **Exports:** Machinery, vehicles, chemicals, iron, steel, textiles, food, wine.
- **Germany** is the world's third biggest industrial nation after the U.S.A. and Japan, famous for its precision engineering and quality products, such as tools and machine tools.
- **Germany's smoky industrial** heartland was the Ruhr valley, where dozens of coal mines fed huge steelworks. Many mines and steelworks have now closed and many people have moved south to places like Stuttgart and Munich to escape unemployment and dirty air.
- **Germany is** the world's third biggest car maker after the U.S.A. and Japan. It is well known for its upscale cars such as Mercedes, BMW, and Audi.
- **German farms** are often small, family-run affairs. Yet the country can grow almost all its own food.

★ STAR FACT ★

The reunification of Germany in 1990 made it western Europe's biggest country by far.

North Africa

- **Morocco:** Capital: Rabat. Population: 28.98 million. Currency: dirham. Language: Arabic.
- **Algeria:** Capital: Algiers. Population: 31.6 million. Currency: Algerian dinar. Language: Arabic.
- **Tunisia:** Capital: Tunis. Population: 9.84 million. Currency: Tunisian dinar. Language: Arabic.
- **Libya:** Capitals: Tripoli and Surt Population: 5.2 million. Currency: Libyan dinar. Language: Arabic.
- **Much of** the world's phosphate supply comes from Morocco and Tunisia.
- **Algeria and Libya** both have large reserves of oil and gas.
- **People in Morocco,** Tunisia, and Algeria eat a lot of couscous. This is made from wheat which is pounded into hard grains of semolina, then steamed until soft. The couscous is then served with stewed lamb or vegetables.
- **The Moroccan** custom is to eat using the right hand rather than knives and forks.
- **The historic cities** of Fez and Marrakesh in Morocco are famous for their colorful *souks* (markets), where thousands of tourists each year come to haggle over beautiful handwoven carpets, leather goods, and jewelry.

★ STAR FACT ★
Libya is building the 2,405mi (3,870km) Great Manmade River, the world's longest water pipe, to irrigate 309 sq mi (800 sq km) of land.

▶ *The countries of northwest Africa have warm, Mediterranean climates and farmers grow produce such as olives and citrus fruits.*

Pacific food

- **Most places** around the Pacific are near the sea, so fish plays an important part in diets.
- **In Japan** fish is usually eaten raw in thin slices called sashimi, or cooked with vegetables in batter as a dish called tempura, served with soy sauce.
- **At home** most Japanese eat traditional foods including rice and noodles, as well as fish, tofu, and vegetables or eggs.
- **When out,** many Japanese people eat American-style foods from fast food restaurants.

▶ *Lightly grilled or barbecued giant prawns and other seafood play a major role in Pacific food.*

- **The Japanese** eat only half as much rice now as they did in 1960, as younger people prefer bread.
- **Younger Japanese** people have a diet richer in protein and fat than their parents', so grow 3–4in (8–10cm) taller.
- **Pacific islanders** traditionally ate fish like bonito and tuna and native plants like breadfruit, coconuts, sweet potatoes, and taro. They made flour from sago palm pith.
- **Many islanders** now eat mainly canned Western food and suffer malnutrition.
- **Filippino** food is a mix of Chinese, Malay, American, and Spanish. *Adobo* is chicken or pork in soy sauce.
- **Some Australians** now often eat "fusion" food which blends Asian with European cooking styles.

London

▲ *London's Houses of Parliament and its tower with its bell, Big Ben, were built in 1858 after a fire destroyed an earlier building.*

- **London** is the capital of the United Kingdom and its largest city by far, with a population of about 7.2 million.
- **People have settled** here for thousands of years, but the city of London began with the Roman city of Londinium.
- **Throughout the 19th century** London was the world's biggest city, with a million people, and the hub of the world's largest empire, the British Empire.
- **London** is based on two ancient cities: the City of London, which developed from the Roman and Saxon towns, and Westminster, which developed around the palaces of English kings around 1,000 years ago.
- **London** has 500,000 factory workers, but most people work in services, such as publishing and other media. London is one of the world's major finance centers.
- **Eight million tourists** come to London each year.
- **London's tallest building** is the Canary Wharf tower which is 800ft (244m) tall.
- **The London Eye** is the biggest wheel in the world, giving people a bird's eye view over London.
- **London's oldest large buildings** are the Tower of London and Westminster Abbey, both 1,000 years old.

★ STAR FACT ★
700,000 people work in banking and finance—more than in any other city in the world.

Iraq and Iran

- **Iran:** Capital: Tehran. Population: 76.4 million. Currency: Iranian rial. Language: Persian (Farsi).
- **Iraq:** Capital: Baghdad. Population: 23.1 million. Currency: Iraqi dinar. Language: Arabic.
- **Iran is the largest** non-Arabic country in the Middle East.
- **Iran was once** called Persia, and was the center of an empire ruled by the Shah that dates back thousands of years. The last Shah was overthrown in 1979.
- **Iran is an Islamic** country, and the strong views of religious leader Ayatollah Khomeini (who died in 1989) played a key role in the revolution in 1979, which brought him to power.

▶ *Iraq and Iran are mostly hot, dry countries, but Iran is much more mountainous, ringed by the Zagros and Elburz mountains.*

- **Iran is famous for its carpets,** often called Persian carpets. They are Iran's second largest export, after oil. Oil brings Iran 80 percent of its export earnings.
- **Iraq** was the place where civilization probably began 7,000 years ago. The Greeks called it Mesopotamia.
- **Since 1979** Iraq has been ruled by Saddam Hussein and his leadership has brought the country into conflict with much of the world, especially when he invaded Kuwait and started the Gulf War in 1991 when the U.S.A. and other nations retaliated.
- **Only about** a sixth of Iraq is suitable for farming and so it has to import much of its food, but it is one of the world's major oil producers.
- **United Nations** sanctions applied after the Gulf War still restrict trade with Iraq. Some argue that it is poor Iraqis who suffer from these and not Saddam Hussein.

West Africa

- **West African countries** are: Cape Verdi, Liberia, Equatorial Guinea, Niger, Mauritania, Mali, Burkina Faso, Senegal, Gambia, Guinea Bissau, Liberia, Guinea, Ivory Coast, Ghana, Sierra Leone, Togo, Benin and São Tomé, and Prîncipe. All have populations under 10 million except for Ghana, Ivory Coast, and Mali.
- **Ghana:** Capital: Accra. Population: 18.4 million. Currency: cedi. Language: English.
- **Ivory Coast:** Capital: Yamoussoukro. Population: 15.14 million. Currency: CFA franc. Language: French.
- **Mali:** Capital: Bamako. Population: 12.56 million. Currency: CFA franc. Language: French.
- **West Africa** grows over half the world's cocoa beans.
- **Yams** are a vital part of the diet of people in West Africa, often providing breakfast, dinner, and tea.
- **West Africa** is rich in gold and diamonds, which once sustained ancient Mali and its capital of Timbuktu.

▲ *Ivory Coast grows 40 percent of the world's cocoa beans. Here beans are drying in the sun.*

- **Ghana and Guinea** are rich in bauxite (aluminum ore).
- **Ghana** was called Gold Coast by Europeans because of the gold used by the Ashanti peoples there.
- **Ghana** is still poor, but many of its young people are the best educated in Africa.

Peoples of North America

- **82 percent** of the population of North America are white descendants of immigrants from Europe.
- **Among the smaller groups,** 13 percent are black, 3 percent are Asian, and 1 percent are Native Americans.
- **Hispanics** are descended from a mix of white, black, and American Indian people from Latin America such as Mexico, Puerto Rico, and Cuba. 12 percent of the U.S. population is Hispanic.
- **92 percent** of the population of the U.S.A. was born here.
- **The original peoples** of North America were the Native Americans who were living here for thousands of years before Europeans arrived.

▲ *Native Americans remain proud of their customs and traditional way of dress.*

- **The native people** of America were called Indians by the explorer Christopher Columbus, but most Native Americans prefer to be identified by tribe.
- **There are about** 540 tribes in the U.S.A.The largest are the Cherokee, Navajo, Chippewa, Sioux, and Choctaw.
- **Most black Americans** are descendants of Africans brought here as slaves from 1600 to 1860.
- **Most European** immigrants before 1820 were from Britain, so the main language is English.
- **Spanish** is spoken by many Americans and French is spoken by 24 percent of Canadians.

The Amazon

- **The Amazon River** in South America is the world's second longest river at 4,007mi (6,448km), and carries far more water than any other river.
- **The Amazon basin,** the area drained by the Amazon and its tributaries, covers nearly 3 million sq mi (7 million sq km) and contains the world's largest tropical rain forest.
- **Temperatures** in the Amazon rain forest stay about 80°F (27°C) all year round.
- **The Amazon rain forest** contains more species of plant and animal than anywhere else in the world.
- **The Amazon is home** to 30,000 different plants, 1,550 kinds of bird, and 3,000 species of fish in its rivers.
- **Manaus** in the Amazon basin has a population of over a million and a famous 19th-century opera house.

★ STAR FACT ★
The Amazon basin is home to more than two million different kinds of insect.

▲ *In its upper reaches in the Andes, the Amazon tumbles over 16,400ft (5,000m) in the first 3,280ft (1,000km).*

- **Since the 1960s** the Brazilian government has been building highways and airports in the forest.
- **Ten percent** of the forest has been lost for ever as trees are cut for wood, or to clear the way for ranching.
- **Forest** can sometimes regrow, but with far fewer species.

Egypt and neighbors

- **Egypt:** Capital: Cairo. Population: 68.12 million. Currency: Egyptian pound. Language: Arabic.
- **Ethiopia:** Capital: Addis Ababa. Population: 66.2 million. Currency: birr. Language: Amharic.
- **Sudan:** Capital: Khartoum. Population: 29.8 million. Currency: Sudanese dinar. Language: Arabic.

- **Egypt relies** heavily on tourists visiting its ancient sites, like the 4,700-year-old Great Pyramid of Cheops at Giza.
- **99 percent of Egyptians** live by the river Nile which provides water for farming, industry, and drinking. A vast reservoir, Lake Nasser, was created when the Nile was dammed by the Aswan High Dam.
- **Cairo** has a population of 11.6 million and is growing so rapidly there are major housing and traffic problems.
- **Lots of cotton** is grown in Egypt and the Sudan.
- **Sudan is the largest** country in Africa.
- **In the 1980s and 1990s** the people of Ethiopia, Sudan, and Somalia suffered dreadful famine. Many people here are still very poor and without enough to eat.
- **Grasslands south of the Sahara** are dotted with acacia thorn trees which ooze a liquid called gum arabic when their bark is cut. This was used in medicine and inks.

◀ *Camels have provided desert transportation in Egypt for thousands of years.*

Australia

- **Capital:** Canberra. Area: 2,966,152 sq mi (7,682,300 sq km). Currency: Australian dollar. Language: English.
- **Physical features:** Highest mountain: Mt. Kosciuszko, 7,316ft (2230m). Longest river: the Murray–Darling, 2330mi (3750km).
- **Population:** 18.84 million. Population density: 5 sq mi (2 sq km). Life expectancy: men 76.8 years; women 82.2 years.
- **Wealth:** GDP: $428.7 billion. GDP per head: $22,755.
- **Exports:** Ores and minerals, coal, oil, machinery, gold, diamonds, meat, textiles, cereals.
- **Australia** enjoyed its own goldrush when gold was discovered in 1851.
- **Most of Australia** is so dry only 2 percent is good for growing crops. But huge areas are used for rearing cattle and sheep, many raised on vast farms called "stations." Australia is also famous for its wines.
- **Australia has huge amounts** of iron, aluminum, zinc, gold, and silver. The Mount Goldsworthy mine in Western Australia alone is thought to have 15 billion tons of iron ore. Broken Hill in New South Wales is the world's largest silver mine.
- **Australia's climate** encourages outdoor activities like surfing. Thousands head for Bondi Beach near Sydney on Christmas Day for a party or to surf. Australia is also the world's top cricketing nation.

The road track across Nullabor Plain is the world's longest straight track

▲ Australia is the world's smallest continent but sixth biggest country. Much of it is dry and thinly populated. Most people live in the southeast or along the coast.

The Great Dividing Range divides the moist coastal plain from the dry outback

★ **STAR FACT** ★

Australia's 115 million sheep produce more than a quarter of the world's wool.

Grand Canyon

- **The Grand Canyon** in Arizona in the southwest U.S.A. is one of the most spectacular gorges in the world.
- **The Grand Canyon** is about 289mi (466km) long and and varies in width from less than 0.6mi (1km) to over 19mi (30km).
- **In places** the Grand Canyon is so narrow that motorcycle stunt riders have leaped right across.
- **The Grand Canyon** is about 5,250ft (1,600m) deep, with almost sheer cliff sides in some places.
- **Temperatures** in the bottom of the Canyon can be as much as 57°F (14°C) hotter than they are at the top, and the bottom of the Canyon gets only 7in (180mm) of rain per year compared to 26in (660mm) at the top.

▲ *The shadows cast by the evening sun reveal the layer upon layer of rock in the steep sides of the Grand Canyon.*

- **The Grand Canyon** was cut by the Colorado River over millions of years as the whole Colorado Plateau was rising bit by bit. The bends in the river's course were shaped when it still flowed over the flat plateau on top, then the river kept its shape as it cut down through the rising plateau.
- **As the Colorado** cut down, it revealed layers of limestone, sandstone, shale, and other rocks in the cliffs.
- **The Colorado** is one of the major U.S. rivers, 1,450mi (2,334km) long.
- **The Hoover Dam** across the Colorado is one of the world's highest concrete dams, 725ft (221m) high.
- **The Hoover Dam** creates 115mi (185km) long Lake Mead, North America's biggest artificial lake.

Peru and neighbors

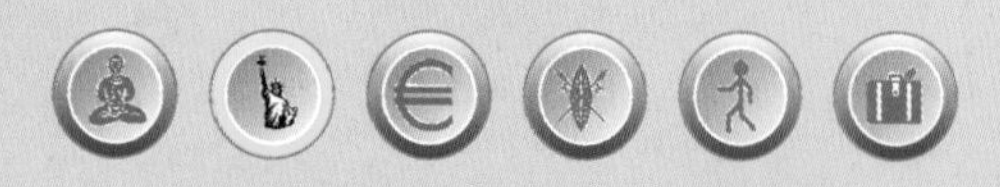

- **Peru:** Capital: Lima. Area: 496,225 sq mi (1,285,216 sq km). Currency: nuevo sol. Languages: Spanish and Quechua.
- **Physical features:** Highest mountain: Huascaran, 22,205ft (6,768m). Longest river: The Amazon, 4,007mi (6,448km).
- **Population:** 25.7 million. Population density: 45 sq mi (20 sq km). Life expectancy: men 65.6 years; women 69.1 years.
- **Wealth:** GDP: $70.18 billion. GDP per head: $2,730.
- **Exports:** Fish products, gold, copper, zinc, iron, oil, coffee, llama and alpaca wool, cotton.
- **Peru** is the third largest country in South America.
- **Peru** was the home of the Inca Empire conquered by the Spaniard Francisco Pizarro in the 1520s. Now it has a larger Indian population than any other South American nation.
- **Peru** is a leading producer of copper, lead, silver, and zinc, and a major fishing nation. But most people are poor, especially in the mountains. In the 1990s guerillas called *Sendero Luminoso* (Shining Path) and *Tupac Amaru* sparked off violent troubles.
- **Ecuador:** Capital: Quito. Population: 12.65 million. Currency: U.S. dollar. Language: Spanish.
- **Bolivia:** Capital: La Paz. Population: 8.3 million. Currency: boliviano. Language: Spanish.

▶ *The llama was for centuries the main source of meat and wool, and the main means of transportation for people in Peru.*

Kenya

- **Capital:** Nairobi. Area: 224,960 sq mi (582,646 sq km). Currency: Kenyan shilling. Languages: Swahili and English.
- **Physical features:** Highest mountain: Mt. Kenya 17,057ft (5,199m). Longest river: Tana 439mi (708km).
- **Population:** 30.3 million (est). Population density: 125 sq mi (52 sq km). Life expectancy: men 47.3 years; women 48.1 years.
- **Wealth:** GDP: $11.46 billion. GDP per head: $380.
- **Exports:** Tea, coffee, fruit, flowers, vegetables, petroleum products.
- **Remains of early human ancestors** found by Lake Turkana show people have lived in Kenya for millions of years.
- **Much of Kenya** is a vast, dry, grassland plain, home to spectacular wildlife such as lions, giraffes, and elephants.
- **Most Kenyans** live on small farm settlements, raising crops and livestock for themselves, but there are big cash crop plantations for tea, coffee, vegetables, and flowers.
- **Many Kenyans** are moving to the big cities: Nairobi and Mombasa.
- **Kenya's population** is growing by 2.5 percent a year.

▼ *The Masai people are just one of about 50 ethnic groups in Kenya.*

Health and education

- **Progress** in medical science, better diet, and improved hygiene have made the world a healthier place for many.
- **How long** people are likely to live is called life expectancy. In 1950, the world average was just 40 years. Now it is over 63 years.
- **Life expectancy** is usually high in richer countries. The Andorrans live on average for 83.5 years; the Japanese live for 80.8 years.
- **Life expectancy** is much lower in poor countries. People in Zambia live just 37.3 years; people in Mozambique live 36.45 years.
- **Vaccination programs** have reduced the effects of some major diseases. The terrible disease smallpox was thought to be wiped out in 1977.
- **Some diseases** are on the increase in poorer parts of the world. AIDS (Acquired Immune Deficiency Syndrome) is now killing huge numbers of Africans.
- **In some parts** of the world, disease, lack of food and water, and poor healthcare mean that one child in four dies before reaching the age of five in poor countries like Afghanistan and Sierra Leone.
- **In the U.S.A. and Europe** fewer than one child in a hundred dies before the age of five.
- **In wealthier** countries such as Italy and Switzerland, there is on average one doctor for every 350 people.
- **In most poor African** countries, there is just one doctor for every 50,000 people.

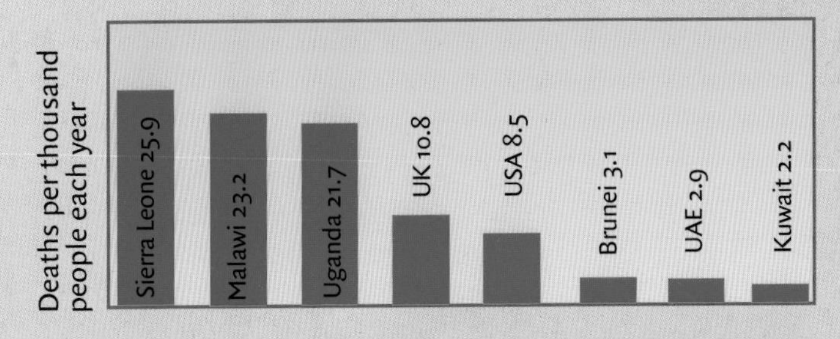

▲ *Death rates per thousand people vary from over 20 in many African countries to under 3 in many Arab countries of the Gulf.*

France

★ STAR FACT ★
French vineyards produce more than 22 percent of the world's wine every year.

- **Capital:** Paris. Area: 210,026 sq mi (543,965 sq km). Currency: euro. Language: French.
- **Physical features:** Highest mountain: Mont Blanc 15,770ft (4,810m). Longest river: the Loire, 625mi (1020km).
- **Population:** 58.74 million. Population density: 262 sq mi (108 sq km). Life expectancy: men 74.9 years; women 83.6 years.
- **Wealth:** GDP: $1,407 billion. GDP per head: $24,330.
- **Exports:** Agricultural products, chemicals, machinery, vehicles, food, and wine.
- **France** is the biggest food producer in Europe, apart from Russia. In the north and west, wheat, sugar beet, and many other crops are grown. Dairy cattle are also raised. In the warmer, drier south of France, grapes and other fruit are grown.

▶ *France is famous both for its beef cattle, like this Charolais, and its dairy cows, which give cheeses including the soft cheeses Brie and Camembert.*

- **France has limited** coal and oil reserves, but nuclear power gives France 75 percent of its energy.
- **France** is the biggest country in western Europe. Much is still rural, with ancient farmhouses and villages looking as if they have changed little in centuries. But French cities like Lyon and Marseilles are famous for their sophisticated culture. They are also the centers of so much industry that France is the world's fifth largest industrial nation after the U.S.A., Japan, Germany, and the U.K.
- **The French** are traditionally famous for their *haute cuisine* (fine cooking) using the best ingredients, and creating fantastic table displays.

▶ *France is a large and enormously varied country. In the center are the rugged hills and volcanic peaks of the Massif Central. To the south is the warm sunny Mediterranean coast. The low, rolling countryside of the north and west is cooler. The highest mountains are the Alps in the southeast and the Pyrenees in the southwest, along the border with Spain.*

Antarctica

- **Antarctica** is the fifth largest continent, larger than Europe and Australia, but 98 percent is under ice.
- **The Antarctic population** is made up mostly of scientists, pilots, and other specialists there to do research in the unique polar environment.
- **About 3,000 people** live in Antarctica in the summer, but fewer than 500 stay all through the bitter winter.
- **The biggest community** in Antarctica is McMurdo which is home to up to 1,200 people in summer and has cafés, a theater, a church, and a nuclear power station.
- **People and supplies** reach McMurdo either on ice-breaker ships that smash through the sea ice, or by air.

- **McMurdo settlement** was built around the hut the British polar explorer Captain Scott put up on his 1902 expedition to the South Pole.
- **The Amundsen–Scott** base is located directly underneath the South Pole.
- **Antarctica** has a few valuable mineral resources including copper and chrome ores.
- **There is coal** beneath the Transarctic Mountains, and oil under the Ross Sea.
- **Under the Antarctic Treaty** of 1961, 27 countries agreed a ban on mining to keep the Antarctic unspoiled. They allow only scientific research.

◀ *Emperor penguins are among the few large creatures that can survive the bitter Antarctic winter. They breed on the ice cap itself.*

Industry

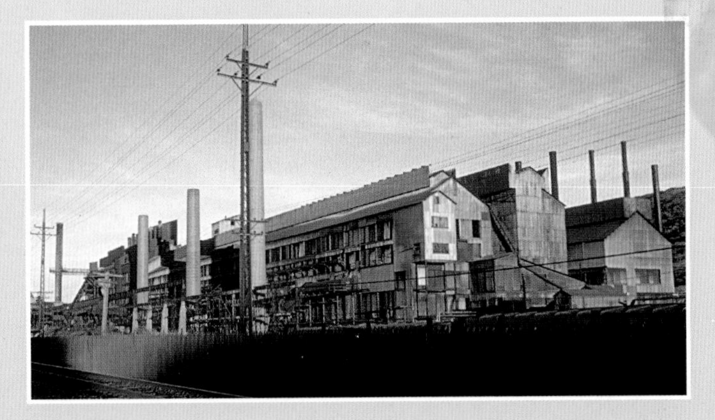

▲ *Nearly every country in the world is becoming increasingly industrialized.*

- **Primary industries** are based on gathering natural resources. They include farming, forestry, fishing, mining, and quarrying.
- **Things made** by primary industries are called primary products or raw materials.
- **Primary industries** dominate the economies of poorer countries. Copper is 80 percent of Zambia's exports.

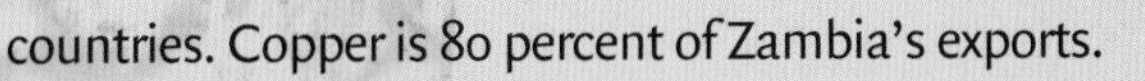

- **Primary products** are much less important in developed countries. Primary products earn 2 percent of Japan's GDP (Gross Domestic Product).
- **Secondary industry** is taking raw materials and turning them into products from knives and forks to jumbo jets. This is manufacturing and processing.
- **Tertiary industries** are the service industries that provide a service, such as banking or tourism, not a product.
- **Tertiary industry** has grown enormously in the most developed countries, while manufacturing has shrunk.
- **"Postindustrialization"** means developing service industries in place of factories.
- **Tertiary industries** include Internet businesses.

★ **STAR FACT** ★
More than 80 percent of the U.S.A.'s income comes from tertiary industry.

The Middle East

- **Saudi Arabia:** Capital: Riyadh. Population: 21.7 million. Currency: riyal. Language: Arabic.
- **Yemen:** Capital: Sana. Population: 18.12 million. Currency: riyal. Language: Arabic.
- **Kuwait:** Capital: Kuwait City. Population: 2.28 million. Currency: Kuwaiti dinar. Language: Arabic.
- **United Arab Emirates (U.A.E.):** Capital: Abu Dhabi. Population: 2.44 million. Currency: dirham. Language: Arabic.
- **Population:** Oman: 2.72 million. Bahrain: 620,000. Qatar: 590,000.
- **Much of the Middle East** is desert. Rub'al Khali in Saudi Arabia lives up to its name, Empty Quarter. Tent-dwelling nomads called Bedouins have herded sheep and goats here for thousands of years. Now most Bedouins live in houses.
- **Oil has made** the Arab states rich. People in the U.A.E., Bahrain, and Kuwait have an income per head on a par with western Europe.
- **Saudi Arabia** is the world's leading exporter of oil and second only to Russia as oil producer. It has 25 percent of the world's known oil reserves.
- **Yemen** is one of the world's poorest countries.
- **The oil-rich states** along the Gulf are short of water. Most comes from wells, but now they are building desalination plants which remove salt water from the ocean.

◀ *Civilization began in the Middle East, but the climate dried and turned much of it to desert.*

The Russian steppes

- **The steppes** are a vast expanse of temperate grassland, stretching right across Asia.
- **"Steppes"** is a word for lowland.
- **The Western Steppe** extends 2,485mi (4,000km) from the plains of the Ukraine through Russia and Kazakhstan to the Altai mountains on the Mongolian border.
- **The steppes** extend 500mi (800km) from north to south.

★ **STAR FACT** ★

The steppes extend 4,970mi (8,000km), a fifth of the way around the world.

- **The Eastern Steppe** extends 1,553mi (2,500km) from the Altai across Mongoliato Manchuria in north China.
- **The Eastern Steppe** is higher and colder than the Western Steppe and the difference between winter and summer is as extreme as anywhere on Earth.
- **Nomadic herders** have lived on the steppes for over 6,000 years.
- **It was on the steppes** near the Black and Caspian Seas that people probably first rode horses 5,000 years ago.
- **The openness** of the steppes meant that travel by horse was easy long before roads were built.

◀ *The steppes have supported nomadic herding people for thousands of years, but their way of life is rapidly dying out.*

American food

▲ *The American hamburger has been spread around the world by fast-food chains. The U.S.A. consumes 45,000 hamburgers every minute!*

- **Many American** foods were brought from Europe by immigrants.
- **Hamburgers** were brought to the U.S.A. in the 1880s by German immigrants, but are now the most famous American food.
- **Frankfurters** came from Frankfurt in Germany (though this is disputed by people from Bavaria). They became known in the U.S.A. as "hot dogs" by the early 1890s.
- **The pizza** came from Naples in Italy, but the first pizzeria opened in New York in 1895. Pizzas caught on after 1945.
- **The bagel** originated in Poland early in the 17th century where it was known as beygl. It was taken to New York by Jewish immigrants and is often eaten filled with smoked salmon and cream cheese.
- **Self-service** cafeterias began in the 1849 San Francisco Gold Rush.
- **The world's first** fast-food restaurant may have been the White Castle which opened in Wichita, Kansas in 1921.
- **The world's biggest** fast-food chain is McDonalds which has more than 29,000 branches worldwide.
- **Pies** have been popular in the U.S.A. since colonial times. Apple pie is the symbol of American home cooking.
- **American home cooking** includes beef steaks, chicken and ham with potatoes plus a salad. But Americans eat out often—not only fast food such as hamburgers and French fries, but Chinese, Italian, and Mexican dishes.

Southern Africa

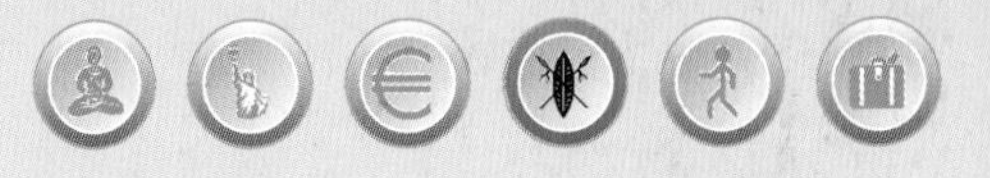

- **Mozambique:** Capital: Maputo. Population: 19.56 million. Currency: Metical. Language: Portuguese.
- **Angola:** Capital: Luanda. Population: 12.78 million. Currency: Kwanza. Language: Portuguese.
- **Zambia:** Capital: Lusaka. Population: 9.87 million. Currency: Kwacha. Language: English.
- **Population:** Namibia: 1.74 million. Botswana: 1.6 million. Swaziland: 985,000.
- **Large areas** of southern African countries are too dry to farm intensively. Most people grow crops such as maize or raise cattle to feed themselves.
- **In Mozambique** plantations grow crops like tea and coffee for export, but most people who work on them are poor.
- **In 2000,** much of Mozambique was devastated by huge floods from the Zambezi and Limpopo Rivers.
- **Zambia is the** world's fourth largest copper producer and relies on copper for 80 percent of its export earnings.
- **Namibia is the** world's second largest lead producer.
- **Namibia** has the world's biggest uranium mine and an estimated three billion carats of diamond deposits.

▼ *The Namib and Kalahari deserts cover much of Namibia and Botswana with sand and dust. Even beyond the deserts, vegetation is sparse and the living poor—except in the mines.*

Tokyo

- **Tokyo** is the world's biggest city. With the port of Yokohama and the cities of Chiba and Kawasaki, it makes an urban area that is home to 27.3 million people.
- **Tokyo** is Japan's capital and leading industrial and financial center.
- **Tokyo's stock exchange** is one of the world's three giants, along with London and New York.
- **Tokyo** was originally called Edo when it first developed as a military center for the Shoguns. It was named Tokyo in 1868 when it became imperial capital.
- **35,000 people** live in every square mile of Tokyo—twice as many as in the same area in New York.
- **Some hotels** in Tokyo have stacks of sleeping cubicles barely bigger than a large refrigerator.

> ★ **STAR FACT** ★
> Tokyo probably has more neon signs than any other city in the world.

▲ *Tokyo is perhaps the busiest, most crowded city in the world.*

- **During rush hours** *osiyas* (pushers) cram people on to commuter trains crowded with 10 million travelers a day.
- **Traffic police** wear breathing apparatus to cope with traffic fumes.
- **Tokyo mixes** the latest western-style technology and culture with traditional Japanese ways.

Canada

- **Capital:** Ottawa. Area: 3,849,674 sq mi (9,970,610 sq km). Currency: Canadian dollar. Languages: English and French.
- **Physical features:** Highest mountain: Mt. Logan, 19,524ft (5,951m). Longest river: the Mackenzie, linked to the Peace by the Great Slave Lake, 2,635mi (4,241km).
- **Population:** 30.68 million. Population density: 8 sq mi (3 sq km). Life expectancy: men 76.2 years; women 81.9 years.
- **Wealth:** GDP: $683.6 billion. GDP per head: $22,280.
- **Exports:** Vehicles and parts, machinery, petroleum, aluminum, timber, wood pulp, wheat.
- **Canada** is the world's second largest country.
- **Three-quarters** of Canada's small population live within 60mi (100km) of the southern border with the U.S.A.
- **Only 5 percent** of Canada is farmed. The Prairie provinces—Saskatchewan, Alberta, and Manitoba—grow a lot of wheat and raise cattle.
- **Canada** has 10 percent of the world's forest and is the world's largest exporter of wood products and paper.
- **The Inuit people** of the far north in the Arctic were given their own homeland of Nunavut in 1999.

◀ *The completion of the Canadian Pacific railroad right across Canada in 1886 was one of the great engineering feats of the 1800s.*

Energy

- **Humans** now use well over 100 times as much energy as they did 200 years ago, and the amount is rising.
- **Europe, North America, and Japan** use 70 percent of the world's energy with just a quarter of the people.
- **Fossil fuels** are coal, oil, and natural gas—fuels made from organic remains buried and fossilized over millions of years. Fossil fuels provide 90 percent of the world's energy.
- **Fossil fuel** pollutes the atmosphere as it burns, causing health problems, acid rain, and also global warming.
- **Fossil fuel** is non-renewable. This means it can't be used again once burned. At today's rates, the world's coal and oil will be burned in 70 years and its natural gas in 220 years.
- **Renewable energy** like running water, waves, wind, and sunlight will not run out. Nuclear energy is non-renewable, but uses far less fuel than fossil fuel.
- **Alternative energy** is energy from sources other than fossil fuels and nuclear power. It should be renewable and clean.
- **Major alternative energy** sources are waves, geothermal, tides, wind, and hydroelectric power.

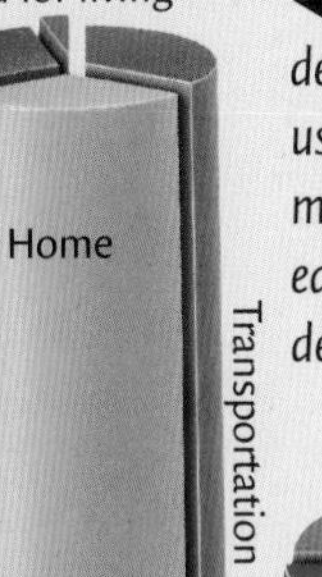

◄▼ *Each person in developed countries uses 10 times as much energy as each person in less developed countries.*

- **The Sun** provides the Earth with about the same as 500 trillion barrels of oil in energy a year—1,000 times as much as the world's oil reserves. Yet little is used. Solar panels provide just 0.01 percent of human energy needs.

★ **STAR FACT** ★
The average American uses 340 times as much energy as the average Ethiopian.

▼ *The pie diagram in the center shows how much of the world's energy is provided by different sources. The top layer shows proportions ten years ago. The bottom layer shows proportions now. See how biomass energy use has risen.*

Oil is our most important energy source, now providing almost 40 percent of the world's energy needs. The biggest reserves are in the Middle East and Central Asia

Coal still provides 23 percent of the world's energy needs. Two-thirds of the world's reserves are in China, Russia, and the U.S.A. India and Australia are major producers too

Wood and dried animal dung, called biomass, provide the main fuel for half the world's population. In some poorer countries, it provides 90 percent of all fuel

Natural gas provides over 22 percent of world energy needs, and the proportion is rising. The biggest reserves are in Russia and the U.S.A.

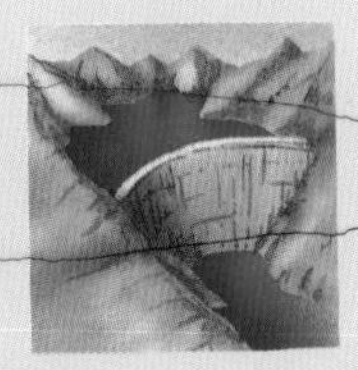

Hydrolectric power (HEP) uses fast-flowing rivers or water flowing through a dam to generate electricity. HEP supplies 7 percent of world energy needs

Nuclear power now provides about 5 percent of the world's energy needs. The major producers are France, the U.S.A., and Russia

Geothermal power uses heat from deep inside the Earth—either to heat water or make steam to generate electricity. Experts think geothermal use will go up

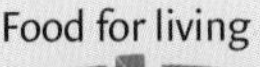

Windpower, wavepower, and solar energy produce barely 5 percent of the world's energy needs. The proportion is going up, but only very, very slowly

Peoples of southern Asia

▶ *Thai people are descended from peoples who migrated from China between the 11th and 12th centuries.*

- **There is a huge** variety of people living in southern Asia from India to the Philippines.
- **India** has hundreds of different ethnic groups speaking 30 languages and 1,652 dialects.
- **Indonesia** also has many different ethnic groups and over 400 different languages and dialects.
- **In Cambodia,** Vietnam, Thailand, Myanmar, and Sri Lanka, people are mostly Buddhists.
- **In Indonesia**, Malaysia, Pakistan, and Bangladesh, people are mostly Muslim.
- **In India,** 81 percent of people are Hindus.
- **The word Hindu** comes from the Indus river where Dravidian people created one of the world's great ancient civilizations 4,500 years ago.
- **By Hindu tradition** people are born into social classes called castes. Members of each caste can only do certain jobs, wear certain clothes, and eat certain food.
- **Most Indians** are descended from both the Dravidians and from the Aryans who invaded and pushed the Dravidians into the south about 3,500 years ago.
- **The people of East Timor** in Indonesia are mainly Christian. Before they became independent they were under the oppressive rule of the Indonesian military government.

Afghanistan & neighbours

- **Afghanistan:** Capital: Kabul. Population: 25.6 million. Currency: Afghani. Language: Pashto, Dari.
- **Tajikistan:** Capital: Dushanbe. Population: 6.4 million. Currency: Tajik rouble. Language: Tajik.
- **Kyrgyzstan:** Capital: Bishkek. Population: 4.54 million. Currency: som. Language: Kyrgyz.
- **Nepal:** Capital: Kathmandu. Population: 24.35 million. Currency: Nepalese rupee. Language: Nepali.
- **These four countries** plus Tibet contain most of the world's highest mountains, including Everest (29,078ft/8,863m), Kanchenjunga (28,209ft/8,598m) in Nepal, and Garmo in Tajikistan (24,590ft/7,495m).
- **The brilliant blue** gemstone lapis lazuli has been mined at Sar-e-Sang in Afghanistan for over 6,000 years.
- **Kyrgyzstan** has been independent from the U.S.S.R. since 1991, but 16 percent of the people are Russian or half-Russian. Only a few still live in the traditional kyrgyz tents or "yurts."
- **Tajikistan** is still mostly rural, unlike Kyrgyzstan, and farmers in the deep valleys grow cotton and melons.
- **Afghanistan** was wracked by war for 17 years until the fiercely Muslim Taliban came to power in the late 1996. Their harsh regime was overthrown in 2001.

▼ *The Himalayas, highlighted on these maps, are the world's highest mountains.*

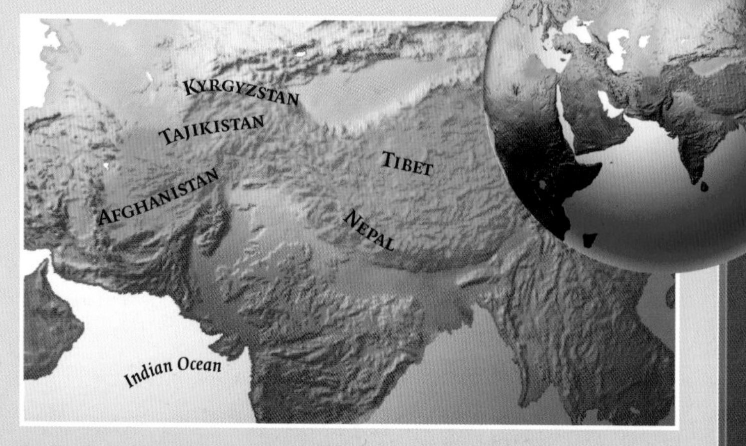

Hungary and neighbors

▲ *Hungary is one of the world's leading producers of sunflower oil, and in summer vast areas of its Great Plain turn yellow with sunflower blooms.*

- **Hungary:** Capital: Budapest. Population: 10.04 million. Currency: Forint. Language: Hungarian.
- **Czech Republic:** Capital: Prague. Population: 10.2 million. Currency: koruna. Language: Czech.
- **Slovakia:** Capital: Bratislava. Population: 5.3 million. Currency: koruna. Language: Slovak.
- **Slovenia:** Capital: Ljubljana. Population: 2 million. Currency: tolar. Language: Slovenian.
- **Until 1990** all of these countries were under Soviet rule except Slovenia. It was part of Yugoslavia.
- **Since 1990**, the historic city of Prague has become a popular destination, especially with the young, and many recording artists have worked in studios here.
- **The Czech Republic** is famous for Pilsen beer brewed in the town of Plzen with hops grown locally.
- **Hungary's** national dish is *goulash*. This is a rich stew made from meat, onion, and potatoes, spiced with paprika (red pepper) and served with black rye bread.
- **Slovakian people** were largely rural, with a strong tradition of folk music, dancing, and dress. Now over half the population has moved into industrial towns.
- **Vienna's white** Lippizaner horses are bred in Slovenia.

Hong Kong

! NEWS FLASH !
The proposed Landmark tower in Kowloon could be 1,889ft (576m) tall.

- **Hong Kong** is a Special Administrative Region on the coast of China. It comprises a peninsula and 237 islands.
- **Hong Kong** was administered by the British from 1842 until July 1, 1997.
- **6.4 million** people are crowded into Hong Kong, mostly in the cities of Kowloon and Hong Kong itself.
- **Hong Kong** is one of the world's most bustling, dynamic, overcrowded cities. It makes huge amounts of textiles, clothing, and other goods and is also one of the world's major financial and trading centers.
- **All but 3 percent** of Hong Kong people are Chinese, but many speak English as well as Chinese.
- **Hong Kong** is one of the world's three biggest ports, along with Rotterdam and Singapore.
- **Hong Kong** is the world's biggest container port.
- **Hong Kong's Chep Lap Kok** airport, opened in 1998, is one of the world's most modern airports.
- **The Hong Kong-Shanghai Bank** tower is one of the world's most spectacular modern office buildings.

▼ *Hong Kong is quite mountainous, so people are crowded on to a small area of land, often in huge, high-rise apartment blocks.*

China

> ★ **STAR FACT** ★
> A baby is born in China every two seconds, and someone dies every two and a half.

- **Capital:** Beijing. Area: 3,696,809 sq mi (9,573,998 sq km). Currency: yuan. Language: Guoy.
- **Physical features:** Highest mountain: Qomolanjma Feng (Mt. Everest), 29,078ft (8,863m). Longest river: Chang Jiang (Yangtse), 3,915mi (6300km).
- **Population:** 1276.2 million. Population density: 331 sq mi (133 sq km). Life expectancy: men 68.1 years; women 71.1 years.
- **Wealth:** GDP: $1,392 billion. GDP per head: $1,000.
- **Exports:** Electrical machinery, textiles and clothing, footwear, toys and games, iron and steel, crude oil, coal, tobacco.
- **China** is the world's third largest country, stretching from the soaring Himalayas in the west to the great plains of the Huang (Yellow) and Chang Jiang (Yangtse) rivers in the east where most people live.
- **China** is the most highly populated country in the world. In 1979, it was growing so rapidly the government made it illegal for couples to have more than one child. In the countryside, people disliked the law because extra children were needed to work the fields. In towns, the law worked better, but single children were often spoiled and so called "Little Emperors."
- **68 percent** of China's people still live and work on the land, growing rice and other crops to feed themselves. But as China opens up to western trade, so industry is growing in cities like Guangzhou (Canton), and more and more country people are going to work there.
- **China** became communist in 1949, and the nationalist government fled to the island of Taiwan. China and Taiwan still disagree over who should govern China. Taiwan now has its own thriving economy and makes more computer parts—especially microchips—than any other country in the world.

▲ With over 1,200 million inhabitants, China has more people than any other country. One in five people alive today are Chinese. China is also one of the world's oldest civilizations and Chinese cities date back at least 4,200 years. People were farming here long before the pharaohs came to power in Egypt.

The island province and city of Hong Kong was ruled by the British from 1842 onward. It was returned to Chinese rule in 1997

▲ Rice is grown all over China in flooded fields called paddies.

Netherlands and Belgium

- **Netherlands:** Capitals: The Hague and Amsterdam. Population: 15.87 million. Currency: euro. Language: Dutch.
- **Belgium:** Capital: Brussels. Population: 10.24 million. Currency: euro. Languages: Flemish and French.
- **Belgium and the Netherlands** are often called the Low Countries because they are both quite flat.The Netherlands' highest hill is just 1,053ft (321m.)
- **A quarter of the Netherlands** (also known as Holland) is polders—land once covered by the sea, but now protected by banks called dikes and pumped dry.
- **The Netherlands** exports more cheese than any other country in the world. Edam and Gouda are famous.
- **The Netherlands** is famous for its vast fields of tulips.

★ STAR FACT ★
The Netherlands is the world's biggest trader in cut flowers.

- **Rotterdam** at the mouth of the Rhine is one of the world's biggest ports, handling a million tons of goods each day.
- **Brussels** is the seat of the European Union Commission and Council.
- **The Belgian** city of Antwerp is the diamond-cutting center of the world.

▶ *Holland is famous for its windmills. These are not for grinding flour but for working the pumps that keep the flat land dry.*

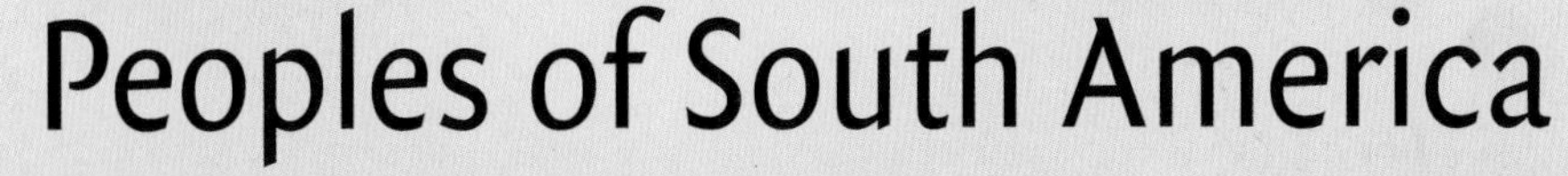

Peoples of South America

- **South America** has a population of a little over 345 million people.
- **Before its conquest** by the Spanish and Portuguese in the 16th century, South America was home to many native peoples.
- **There are native villages** in the Andes with only one race, and a few native tribes in the Amazon rain forest who have had little contact with the outside world.
- **The main population groups now** are American Indians, whites, blacks (whose ancestors were brought as slaves), and people of mixed race.

▶ *In the Amazon, small tribes like the Matses still survive as they have done for thousands of years.*

- **Most people** in Latin America are mixed race.
- **The largest mixed race** groups are *mestizos* (people with both American Indian and white ancestors) and *mulattoes* (people with black and white ancestors).
- **Mestizos** are the majority in countries such as Paraguay and Venezuela. Mulattoes are the majority in Brazil.
- **The Europeans** who came to South America were mostly Spanish and Portuguese, so nearly two-thirds of South Americans speak Spanish.
- **Many American Indians** speak their own languages.
- **Quechua** is a native language, which Peru has made its official language along with Spanish.

Midwest U.S.A.

- **Huge amounts** of wheat and corn are grown on the damper eastern side of the vast rolling plains.
- **Millions** of beef cattle are raised on ranches in the drier west.
- **The weather is often extreme** here with scorching summer days and winter blizzards.
- **Tornado Alley** is a band through Kansas and beyond which is blasted by hundreds of tornadoes every summer.
- **Heavy farming** in the 1930s let dry winds strip away soil leaving just dust over a vast area called the Dust Bowl. Irrigation and windbreaks have lessened the problem.
- **Millions of buffalo (bison)** roamed the Great Plains 200 years ago. Now just 50,000 live on reserves.

◀ The Midwest is North America's agricultural heartland, raising millions of cattle and growing vast areas of yellow corn.

- **Detroit** on the Great Lakes is the center of the U.S. car industry. Ford, Chrysler, and General Motors all have their headquarters here.
- **Detroit** is sometimes known as Motown (short for "motor town") and was famous in the 1960s for its black soul "Motown" music.
- **Many Italians** have emigrated to the U.S.A. and most U.S. cities have an Italian area. Chicago's Italians invented their own deep, soft version of the pizza.
- **Chicago,** known as "The Windy City," is the U.S.A.'s third largest city, home to over nine million people.

Ireland

- **Capital:** Dublin. Area: 271,136 sq mi (70,282 sq km). Currency: euro. Languages: Irish and English. Over two-thirds of Ireland is in the Republic of Ireland. The rest is Northern Ireland which is part of the U.K.
- **Physical features:** Highest mountain: Carrauntoohil, 3,415ft (1041m). Longest river: the Shannon, 231mi (372km).
- **Population (Republic):** 3.71 million. Population density: 132 sq mi (53 sq km). Life expectancy: men 73.8 years; women 79.4 years.

◀ Right out on the northwest of Europe in the Atlantic, Ireland is a mild, moist place. Damp mists and frequent showers keep grass lush and green, earning the island the name "The Emerald Isle."

- **Wealth (Republic):** GDP: $99.8 billion. GDP per head: $26,880.
- **Exports:** Machinery and transportation equipment, chemicals.
- **Peat** is one of Ireland's few natural energy resources. Peat is the compressed rotten remains of plants found in peat bogs. Once dried it can be burned as fuel.
- **Ireland** is famous for its pubs, folk music, and hospitality.
- **Ireland**, Dublin in particular, has been thriving in recent years—partly because of the success of high tech electronics and computer industries.
- **Entertainment** is big business in Ireland—cinema, pop, rock, and folk music are huge money earners.

★ STAR FACT ★

Ireland has enjoyed the fastest growing economy in Europe since the mid 1990s.

North and South Korea

- **North Korea:** Capital: Pyongyang. Population: 22.17 million. Currency: won. Language: Korean.
- **South Korea:** Capital: Seoul. Population: 46.1 million. Currency: won. Language: Korean.
- **Korea** split into the communist North and capitalist South in 1948.
- **A bitter war** between North and South involving the U.S.A. ended with a treaty in 1953.
- **North and South Korea** both still have large armies. South Korea's has over half a million soldiers.
- **After the war,** money from U.S. banks helped the South, for a time, to become the world's fastest growing economy.
- **Huge factories** run by companies called *chaebol* churned out everything from computers to Hyundai and Daewoo cars.
- **South Korean shipyards** build one in six of the world's ships. Only Japan builds more.
- **Since 1997** North Korea has suffered food shortages after two years of floods followed by drought.
- **In 1997–98** the uncovering of massive government dishonesty made many South Korean businesses bankrupt. President Kim Dae Jung has led a recovery. Korea, along with Japan, hosted the 2002 World Cup football tournament.

◀ *The Korean company of Daewoo not only makes cars, but ships, computers, TVs, videos, and much more.*

Central Africa

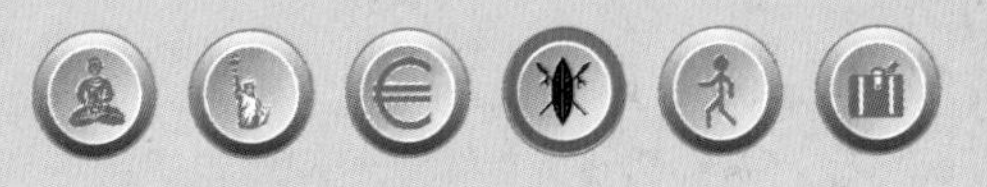

- **Equatorial Guinea:** Capital: Malabo. Population: 450,000. Currency: CFA franc. Languages: Fang and Spanish.
- **Gabon:** Capital: Libreville. Population: 1.23 million. Currency: CFA franc. Language: French.
- **Congo (Brazzaville):** Capital: Brazzaville. Population: 3 million. Currency: CFA franc. Languages: Monokutuba and French.
- **Cameroon:** Capital: Yaoundé. Population: 15.3 million. Currency: CFA franc. Languages: Fang, French, and English.
- **Central African Republic (C.A.R.):** Capital: Bangui. Population: 3.64 million. Currency: CFA franc. Languages: Sango and French.
- **French and English** are official languages, but most people speak their own African language.
- **Most Gabonese** are farmers, but Gabon is rich in oil, iron, and manganese, and famous for its ebony and mahogany.
- **70 percent of people** in Cameroon are farmers, growing crops such as cassava, corn, millet, yams, and sweet potatoes. Most of Cameroon's roads are dust roads.
- **Congo (Brazzaville)** is so called to distinguish it from neighboring D.R. Congo. It is one of the world's poorest countries. It is thickly forested and many people travel by dugout canoes. Many raise bananas or grow crops to feed themselves.
- **The C.A.R. and Equatorial Guinea** are among the least developed countries in Africa.

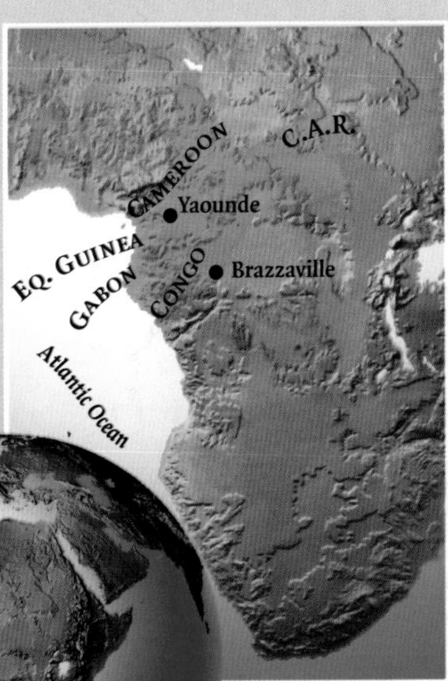

▶ *Cameroon, Gabon, C.A.R., Congo, and Equatorial Guinea lie near the Equator*

Nigeria and neighbors

- **Nigeria:** Capital: Abuja. Population: 128.8 million. Currency: naira. Languages: include English Creole, Hausa, Yoruba, English.
- **Niger:** Capital: Niamey. Population: 10.8 million. Currency: CFA franc. Languages: Hausa, French.
- **Chad:** Capital: N'Djamena. Population: 7.27 million. Currency: CFA franc. Languages: Arabic and French.
- **Most people** in the north of Nigeria, and in Niger and Chad live by growing food for themselves.
- **The amount of rainfall** increases dramatically from north to south, and the vegetation changes from rain forest to dry grassland to desert in marked bands.
- **In the dry north,** people grow mainly millet; in the moist south, they grow rice and roots such as cassava and yam.
- **Oil makes up 95 percent** of Nigeria's exports.
- **The money from oil** has made Nigeria among the most heavily urbanized and populous countries in Africa, especially around its main city Lagos.
- **Nigeria** is home to over 250 different peoples.
- **Nigeria** became a democracy again in 1998 after years of bitter civil war and military dictatorship, but tensions remain.

▼ *The position of Nigeria, Niger, and Chad on the southern fringes of the Sahara Desert makes them prone to drought as climate change and overgrazing push the desert farther south.*

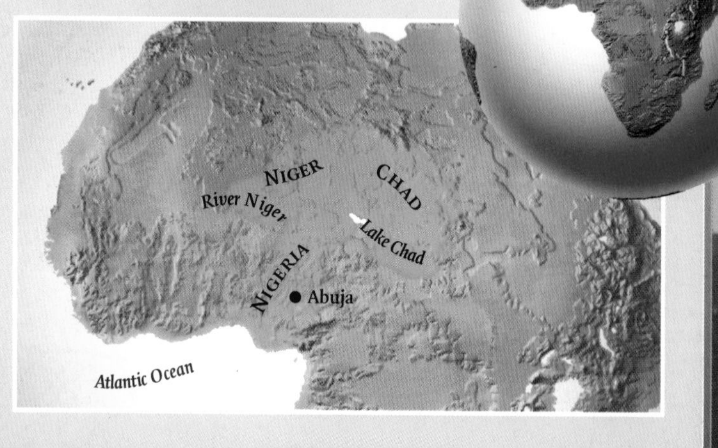

Argentina

▼ *"Gaucho" means orphan, but the tough gauchos are Argentina's heroes.*

- **Capital:** Buenos Aires. Area: 1,068,302 sq mi (2,766,889 sq km). Currency: peso. Language: Spanish.
- **Physical Features:** Highest mountain: Aconcagua, 22,835ft (6,960m). Longest river: Paraná, 2,450mi (4,880km).
- **Population:** 37.03 million. Population density: 32 sq mi (13 sq km). Life expectancy: men 69.7 years; women 76.8 years.
- **Wealth:** GDP: $367 billion. GDP per head: $9,900.
- **Exports:** Wheat, maize, meat, hides, wool, tannin, linseed oil, peanuts, processed foods, minerals.
- **Argentina's landscape** is dominated by the pampas, vast, flat grasslands which stretch all the way to the high Andes mountains in the west.
- **Most of Argentina's** exports are pampas products—wheat, corn, meat, hides, and wool.
- **Cattle** on the pampas—there are 49 million of them.
- **Argentina** is South America's most educated country.

★ STAR FACT ★

Argentineans eat more meat than any other nation in the world.

The United Kingdom

- **Capital:** London. Area: 93,643 sq mi (244,088 sq km). Currency: pound. Language: English.
- **Physical features:** Highest mountain: Ben Nevis, 4,400ft (1,343 m). Longest river: Severn, 219mi (354km).
- **Population:** 59.73 million. Population density: 599 sq mi (245 sq km). Life expectancy: men 74.5 years; women 79.8 years.
- **Wealth:** GDP: $1,450 billion. GDP per head: $24,280.
- **Exports:** Manufactured goods such as chemicals and electronics, financial services, music, and publishing.
- **The British Isles** are 4,000 islands with 12,500mi (20,000km) of coast. There are two large islands: Great Britain and Ireland. The United Kingdom (U.K.) is four countries joined politically—England, Scotland, Wales, and Northern Ireland.
- **England** is intensively farmed, especially in the south where wheat, barley, rape, sugar beet, and vegetables are grown. In the moister west and north of England, especially, and Scotland and Wales, cattle and sheep are reared.
- **The Industrial Revolution** began in the U.K. in the 1800s. Heavy industries such as steelmaking and engineering grew in northern coalfield cities like Manchester and Leeds. Now coal's importance as an energy source has dwindled, and some smaller northern towns are finding it difficult to survive. But southern England is thriving on light industries and services.
- **London** is one of the world's great financial centers. Over 500 international banks are crammed into a small area of the city called the Square Mile. Here billions of dollars' worth of money deals are done every day.

▲ The Millennium Dome was erected by the River Thames in east London to celebrate the year 2000.

SCOTLAND
Ben Nevis
Grampian Mountains
Atlantic Ocean
EDINBURGH
Glasgow
Southern Uplands
North Sea
N. IRELAND
BELFAST
Irish Sea
Manchester
Liverpool
DUBLIN
IRELAND
Cambrian Mts
St. George's Channel
Birmingham
WALES
ENGLAND
Cork
Bristol
CARDIFF
LONDON
Dover
English Channel
Plymouth

◀ England is the biggest and most densely populated of the countries of the U.K.—a lush land of rolling hills, rich farmland, and big cities. Wales is a land of hills and sheep farms, except for the south where industry is important and coal was once mined in huge amounts. Much of Scotland is wild, and most people live in the central lowlands around the cities of Glasgow and Edinburgh. A third of Northern Ireland's population lives in Belfast.

★ STAR FACT ★

Over 60 percent of the U.K.'s workforce work in financial and service industries.

The Near East

- **Syria:** Capital: Damascus. Population: 16.13 million. Currency: Syrian pound. Language: Arabic.
- **Jordan:** Capital: Amman. Population: 5.23 million. Currency: Jordan dinar. Language: Arabic.
- **Lebanon:** Capital: Beirut. Population: 3.29 million. Currency: Lebanese pound. Language: Arabic.
- **Damascus** was a major trading center 4,000 years ago.
- **Syria** is at the western end of the belt of rich farmland known as the fertile crescent, which was the cradle of the earliest civilizations, along the banks of the Tigris and Euphrates rivers.
- **Most Syrian farmers** still work on small plots growing cotton and wheat. But 40 percent of Syrians now work in services.
- **Around 70 percent of Jordan's** income is from services like tourism and banking.
- **The people of Syria,** Jordan, and Lebanon are mostly Arabs. 90 percent of Syrians and Jordanians are Muslims, but 35 percent of Lebanese are Christians.
- **In 1948** Palestine was split between Israel, Jordan, and Egypt. Palestinian Arabs' desire for their own country has caused conflict with Israelis.
- **In 1996** Israeli troops withdrew from the Gaza strip. Palestinians elected their own local administration.

Indian food

- **Most Indians** live on very plain diets—based on staples such as rice in the east and south, *chapatis* (flat wheat bread) in the north and northwest, and *bajra* (millet bread) in the Maharashtra region.
- **The staple foods** are supplemented by *dal* (lentil porridge), vegetables, and yogurt.
- **Chilies and other spices** such as coriander, cumin, ginger, and turmeric add flavor.
- **Chicken and mutton** are costly and eaten occasionally. Hindus will not eat beef and Muslims will not eat pork.
- **Many Indian meals** are cooked in *ghee* (liquid butter). Ghee is made by heating butter to boil off water, then allowing it to cool and separate. Ghee is scooped off the top.
- **Although many Indians** have simple diets, India has an ancient and varied tradition of fine cooking.
- **Curries are** dishes made with a sauce including the basic spices turmeric, cumin, coriander, and red pepper. The word curry comes from the Tamil *kari*, or sauce.
- **The basis of a curry** is a *masala*, a mix of spices, often blended with water or vinegar to make a paste.
- **Southern Indian** vegetable curries are seasoned with hot blends like *sambar podi*.
- **Classic northern Indian** Mughal dishes are often lamb, or chicken based, and seasoned with milder *garam masala*.

◀ *An Indian meal is rarely served on a single plate. Instead, it comes in different dishes, which diners dip into.*

Paris

▲ *Les Halles was the main market for Paris from the 12th century, but in the 1970s was transformed into a modern shopping center.*

- **Paris** is the capital of France and its largest city with a population of over nine million.
- **Paris** is France's main business and financial center. The Paris region is also a major manufacturing region, notably for cars.
- **Paris** is famed for luxuries like perfume and fashion.
- **Paris** is known for restaurants like La Marée, cafés like Deux Magots, and nightclubs like the Moulin Rouge.
- **Paris** monuments include the Arc de Triomphe, the Eiffel Tower, Notre Dame cathedral and the Beauborg Centre.
- **Paris** gets its name from a Celtic tribe called the Parisii who lived there 2,000 years ago.
- **The Roman general** Julius Caesar said the Parisii were "clever, inventive and given to quarreling among themselves." Some say this is true of Parisians today.
- **Paris** was redeveloped in the 1850s and 60s by Baron Haussman on the orders of Emperor Napoleon III.
- **Haussman** gave Paris broad, tree-lined streets called boulevards, and grand, gray, seven-story houses.

★ **STAR FACT** ★

Well over half of France's business deals are done in Paris.

Balkan peninsula

- **The Balkan peninsula** is a mountainous region in southeast Europe.
- **The Balkans** include different nations—some were under the Austro-Hungarian or Turkish Empires until 1918.
- **In 1945 Yugoslavia** became six republics in a federal Communist state. This ended in 1991.
- **Bosnia-Herzegovina,** Croatia, Macedonia, Slovenia, and Kosovo broke away from Yugoslavia in the 1990s amid much bitter conflict.
- **Serbia and Montenegro** formed a smaller Yugoslavia in 1992. This ceased to exist in May 2002 when the country was reformed as Serbia and Montenegro.
- **Serbia and Montenegro**: Capital: Belgrade. Population: 10.5 million. Currency: dinar (Serbia), euro (Montenegro). Language: Serb.
- **Croatia:** Capital: Zagreb. Population: 4.48 million. Currency: kuna. Language: Croat.
- **Bosnia-Herzegovina:** Capital: Sarajevo. Population: 4.3 million. Currency: dinar. Languages: Serb and Croat.
- **Albania:** Capital: Tirana. Population: 3.49 million. Currency: new lek. Language: Albanian.
- **Macedonia:** Capital: Skopje. Population: 2.23 million. Currency: dinar. Languages: Macedonian, Albanian.

▼ *This bridge at Mostar in Bosnia-Herzegovina was a casualty of the wars of the 1990s.*

Agriculture

Millet
Sweet Potato
Barley
Potato
Rice
Corn
Casava
Wheat
Oats
Soya Bean

▶ Most of the world's food is grown in the Northern Hemisphere or Asia. Asia is a major grower of wheat, rice, sweet potatoes, sorghum, and all pulses such as beans. In fact, 90 percent of all rice and sweet potatoes are grown in Asia. Half the world's corn is grown in North America. 40 percent of potatoes are grown in Europe.

★ STAR FACT ★
There are now over twice as many farm animals in the world as humans—over 14 billion.

- **Only 12 percent** of the Earth's ice-free land surface is suitable for growing crops—that is, about 32 billion acres (13 billion hectares). The rest is either too wet, too dry, too cold, too steep, or the soil is too shallow or poor.
- **A much higher** proportion of Europe has fertile soil (36 percent) than any other continent. About 31 percent is cultivated.
- **In North America** 22 percent of the land is fertile but only 13 percent is cultivated, partly because much fertile land is lost under concrete. 16 percent of Africa is potentially fertile, yet only 6 percent is cultivated.
- **Southern Asia** is so crowded that although less than 20 percent of the land is fertile, over 24 percent is cultivated.
- **Dairy farms** produce milk, butter, and cheese from cows in green pastures in fairly moist parts of the world.
- **Mixed farming** involves both crops and livestock, as in the U.S.A.'s Corn Belt, where farmers grow corn to feed pigs and cattle. Many European farms are mixed, too.
- **Mediterranean farming** is in areas with mild, moist winters and warm, dry summers, such as California and the Mediterranean. Here winter crops include wheat and barley. Summer crops include citrus fruits and olives.
- **Shifting cultivation** involves growing crops like corn, rice, manioc, yams, and millet in one place for a short while, then moving on before the soil loses fertility.
- **Shifting cultivation** is practiced in the forests of Latin America, in Africa, and parts of Southeast Asia.

◀ In places, farming is now highly mechanized, but in Southeast Asia many farmers work the land as they have for thousands of years.

The West Indies

▶ *Famous Jamaica rum is made from cane sugar, still the West Indies' major crop despite the rise of beet sugar.*

- **Cuba:** Capital: Havana. Population: 11.2 million. Currency: Cuban peso. Language: Spanish.
- **Jamaica:** Capital: Kingston. Population: 2.59 million. Currency: Jamaican dollar. Language: English.
- **The four largest islands** in the West Indies are Cuba, Hispaniola, Jamaica, and Puerto Rico. Hispaniola is split into two countries: Haiti and the Dominican Republic.
- **The islands** are mostly in a long curve stretching from Cuba to Trinidad. The Greater Antilles are the islands of the western end. The Lesser Antilles are the eastern end.
- **The original inhabitants** of the West Indies were Carib and Arawak peoples. Most died soon after the Spanish arrived in the 1500s from disease and abuse.
- **Today most West Indians** are descended from Africans brought here as slaves to work on the sugar plantations.
- **The slaves** were freed in the mid to late 1800s, but most people here are still poor and work for low wages.
- **In Haiti** only one person in 250 has a car; fewer than one in ten has a phone.
- **Many people** work the land on sugar, banana, or coffee plantations, and also farm a patch to grow their own food.
- **Many tourists** come for the warm weather and clear blue seas.

Vietnam and neighbors

- **Vietnam:** Capital: Hanoi. Population: 80.5 million. Currency: dong. Language: Vietnamese.
- **Laos:** Capital: Vientiane. Population: 5.6 million. Currency: kip. Language: Lao.
- **Cambodia:** Capital: Phnom Penh. Population: 12.5 million. Currency: riel. Language: Khmer.
- **Indonesia:** Capital: Jakarta. Population: 212.6 million. Currency: rupiah. Main language: Bahasa Indonesia.

◀ *Warm and damp, Southeast Asia is a fertile region where Buddhist and Hindu kings once built giant temples in the forests, but many people today are desperately poor.*

- **Laos, Vietnam, and Cambodia** were once French colonies and the end of French rule in the 1950s led to years of suffering and war.
- **Both Laos and Vietnam** are one-party communist states, although their governments are elected by popular vote. In Cambodia, the king was reinstated in 1993.
- **Many people** in Laos and Vietnam are poor and live by growing rice. Laos is the world's poorest country.
- **In Indonesia**, an elected president has replaced dictator General Suharto, but the military still has great power.
- **Spread over 13,700 islands,** Indonesia is one of the world's most densely populated countries. Jakarta is home to 12.4 million, and is heavily industrialized. In the country hillside terraces ensure every inch is used for rice.
- **Indonesian rain forest** is being rapidly destroyed by loggers. In 1997, parts of the country were engulfed by smoke from fires started by loggers.

Malaysia and Singapore

- **Malaysia:** Capitals: Kuala Lumpur and Putrajaya. Pop: 22.3 million. Currency: Malaysian dollar (ringgit). Language: Bahasa Malaysia.
- **Singapore:** Capital: Singapore. Population: 4.01 million. Currency: Singapore dollar. Languages: English, Mandarin, Malay, and Tamil.
- **Malaysia** is split into sections: peninsular Malaysia and Sarawak and Sabah on the island of Borneo.
- **In the 1980s** Malaysia was a farming country relying on rubber for exports.
- **Malaysia** is still the world's top rubber producer.
- **Cheap, skilled labor** and oil have turned Malaysia into one of the world's most rapidly developing economies.
- **A plan called 2020 Vision** aims to have Malaysia fully developed by the year 2020.
- **Singapore** may be the world's busiest port. Huge ships tie up here every three minutes.
- **Singapore** is also one of Asia's most successful trading and manufacturing centers.
- **Singapore** has a state-of-the-art transportation system, kept immaculately clean by strict laws governing litter.

▲ *Singapore is one of the busiest and most prosperous cities in Asia.*

Peoples of Europe

- **About 730 million** people live in Europe—about 12 percent of the world's population.
- **Europe** is one of the most densely populated continents averaging 174 people per square mile.
- **Most Europeans** are descended from tribes who migrated into Europe more than 1,500 years ago.

◄ *In Eastern Europe, many people, like this Romanian, have their own traditional dress.*

- **Most British people** are descended from a mix of Celts, Angles, Saxons, Danes, and others. Most French people are descended from Gauls and Franks. Most Eastern Europeans are Slavic (see peoples of Northern Asia).
- **North Europeans** such as Scandinavians often have fair skin and blonde hair. South Europeans such as Italians often have olive skin and dark hair.
- **Most European countries** have a mix of people from all parts of the world, including former European colonies in Africa and Asia.
- **Most Europeans** are Christians.
- **Most Europeans** speak an Indo-European language, such as English, French, or Russian.
- **Languages** like French, Spanish, and Italian are romance languages that come from Latin, language of the Romans.
- **Basque people** in Spain speak a language related to no other language. Hungarians, Finns, and Estonians speak a Finno-Ugrian language.

Chile

- **Capitals:** Santiago and Valparaiso. Area: 292,156 sq mi (756,626 sq km). Currency: Chilean peso. Language: Spanish.
- **Physical features:** Highest mountain: Ojos del Solado, 22,621ft (6,895m). Longest river: Bio-Bio, 236mi (380km).
- **Population:** 15.21 million. Population density: 50 sq mi (20 sq km). Life expectancy: men 72.4 years; women 78.4 years.
- **Wealth:** GDP: $95 billion. GDP per head: $6,240.
- **Exports:** Copper, iron, fresh fruit, wood pulp.
- **Chile** is one of the world's most volcanically active countries, with 75 active volcanoes. Chile also has eight of the world's highest active volcanoes.
- **Chile is a major** wine producer.
- **The copper mine** at Chuquicamata is the world's biggest manufactured hole.
- **Chile is the** world's largest copper producer.
- **The Mapuche Indians** live in the forest area around Temuco in southern Chile and those who preserve their traditional way of life live in round straw houses.

▶ *Chile is very long and narrow—2,653mi (4,270 km) long and less than 112mi (180km) wide.*

Spain and Portugal

- **Spain:** Capital: Madrid. Area: 195,378 sq mi (505,990 sq km). Currency: euro. Language: Spanish.
- **Physical features:** Highest mainland mountain: Mulhacén, 11,410ft (3,478m). Longest river: Tagus, 625mi (1,007km).
- **Population:** 39.5 million. Population density: 177 sq mi (71 sq km). Life expectancy: men 74.7 years; women 81.6 years.
- **Wealth:** GDP: $5,692.5 billion. GDP per head: $14,990.
- **Exports:** Cars, machinery, wine, fruit, steel, textiles.
- **Much of the center of Spain** is too hot and dry for some crops, but perfect for olives, sunflowers, and for grapes, oranges, and other fruit.
- **Spain is one of the leading** carmakers in Europe, with huge plants in Valencia and Saragossa. It also makes a lot of iron and steel.
- **Portugal:** Capital: Lisbon. Population: 9.79 million. Currency: euro. Language: Portuguese.
- **Portugal** once had a large empire including large parts of Latin America and Africa. Yet it is fairly underdeveloped. Most people still live in the countryside, growing wheat, rice, almonds, olives, and corn.

◀ *Spain and Portugal are isolated from the rest of Europe by the Pyrenees on their own peninsula, called Iberia. Mainland Europe's most westerly point, Cabo da Roca, is in Portugal.*

★ STAR FACT ★
Every summer, 63 million sunseekers come to Spain's beaches and islands.

Scandinavia

▲ *Norway's mountainous coast has been gouged into deep fjords by glaciers.*

- **Norway:** Capital: Oslo. Population: 4.48 million. Currency: Norwegian krone. Language: Norwegian.
- **Sweden:** Capital: Stockholm. Population: 8.9 million. Currency: Swedish krona. Language: Swedish.
- **Denmark:** Capital: Copenhagen. Population: 5.33 million. Currency: Danish krone. Language: Danish.
- **Finland:** Capital: Helsinki. Population: 5.2 million. Currency: euro. Languages: Finnish and Swedish.
- **Scandinavia** has among the iciest, most northerly inhabited countries in the world. Yet they enjoy a high standard of living and welfare provision.
- **Norway's fishing boats** land 2.4 million tons of fish a year—more than those of any other European country except Russia.

- **Sweden is known** for its high-quality engineering, including its cars such as Volvos and aircraft-makers such as Saab.
- **Finland and Sweden** are known for their glass and ceramic work.
- **Sweden's capital Stockholm** is built on 14 islands in an archipelago comprising thousands of islands.
- **Danish farms** are famous for butter and bacon.

Political systems

▶ *Bill Clinton was President of the U.S.A. from 1992 to 2000.*

- **Democracies** are countries with governments elected every few years by popular vote.
- **Most democracies** have a constitution, a written set of laws saying how a government must be run.
- **Democracies** like France are republics. This means the head of state is an elected president. In some republics like the U.S.A., the president is in charge; in others, the president is a figurehead and the country is run by a prime minister.
- **Monarchies** are countries which still have a monarch—a king or queen—like Britain. But their power is usually limited and the country is run by an elected government.
- **In autocracies** a single person or small group of people hold all the power, as in China and North Korea.
- **Most governments** are split into the legislature who make or amend laws, the executive who put them into effect, and the judiciary who see they are applied fairly.
- **Most countries** are capitalist, which means most things —capital—are owned by individuals or small groups.
- **A few countries** like Cuba are communist, which means everything is owned by the community, or rather the state.
- **Socialists** believe the government should ensure everyone has equal rights, a fair share of money, and good health, education, and housing.
- **Fascists** believe in rigid discipline and that they and their country are superior to others, like Hitler's Germany in the 1930s. There is no openly fascist country at present.

The Pacific Islands

- **Scattered** around the Pacific are countless islands—approximately 25,000. Some are little more than rocks; some are thousands of square miles.
- **The Pacific Islands** are in three main groups: Melanesia, Micronesia, and Polynesia.
- **Melanesia** includes New Guinea, the Solomons, New Caledonia, Vanuatu, and Fiji.

- **Melanesia** means "black islands" and gets its name from the dark skin of many of the islanders here.
- **Micronesia** is 2,000 islands to the north of Melanesia, including Guam and the Marshall Islands.
- **Micronesia** means "tiny island."
- **Polynesia** is a vast group of islands 4,970mi (8,000km) across. It includes Tahiti, Samoa, Tonga, Kiribati, and Easter Island.
- **Polynesia** means "many islands."
- **Most of the islands** in the Pacific are either extinct volcanoes, or coral islands built around a volcanic peak. Atolls are coral rings left as the volcano sinks.
- **Most Pacific islanders** still live in small farming or fishing villages as they have for thousands of years, but western influences are changing the island way of life rapidly.

◀ *Like many Pacific islands, Fiji seems like a paradise.*

Mexico

- **Capital:** Mexico City. Area: 761,604 sq mi (1,958,201 sq km). Currency: Mexican peso. Language: Spanish.
- **Physical features:** Highest mountain: Citlaltépetl, 18,900ft (5,700m). Longest river: Rio Bravo, 1,886mi (3,035km).
- **Population:** 97.01 million. Population density: 125 sq mi (50 sq km). Life expectancy: men 69.7 years; women 75.7 years.
- **Wealth:** GDP: $469.5 billion. GDP per head: $4,840.
- **Exports:** Petroleum, vehicles, machinery, cotton, coffee, fish, fertilizers, minerals.
- **Mexico** is quite mountainous and only 13 percent of the land is suitable for farming. Where there is enough rain, there are big plantations for tobacco, coffee, cane, cocoa, cotton, and rubber.
- **Over half Mexico's** export earnings come from manufactured goods—notably cars.
- **Mexico has** a rapidly growing population. Birth rate is high and half the population is under 25.
- **Most of Mexico's people** are *mestizos*—descended from both American Indians and Europeans. But there are still 29 million American Indians.
- **Mexico City** is one of the world's biggest, busiest, dirtiest cities. The urban area has a population of over 18.4 million.

◀ *Mexico lies immediately south of the U.S.A., between the Gulf of Mexico and the Pacific.*

Mediterranean food

- **Mediterranean food** depends on ingredients grown in the warm Mediterranean climate. It tends to be lighter than north European food, including salads, flat bread, and fish rather than sauces and stews.

◀ *Spaghetti Bolognese—spaghetti pasta with meat and tomato sauce—is the centerpiece of a typical Italian meal.*

- **Olive oil** is used for dressing salads and frying food.
- **There are several styles** of Mediterranean food, such as Italian, Greek, Turkish, and Spanish.
- **Italian meals** often include pasta, which is made from durum wheat flour and served with a sauce.
- **Popular forms of pasta** include spaghetti ("little strings"), vermicelli ("little worms"), fusilli ("spindles"), and tube-shaped macaroni.
- **In north Italy**, ribbon pastas served with cream sauces are popular. In the south, macaroni served with tomato-based sauces are more popular.
- **Pizzas** are popular snacks, especially in the south.
- **Greek food** includes meats—especially lamb—and fish cooked in olive oil.
- **Greek salad** includes olives, cucumber, tomatoes, herbs, and feta cheese (soft goat's cheese).
- **Spanish food** often includes seafood such as *calamares* (squid). *Paella* includes seafoods and chicken combined with rice and cooked in saffron. *Gazpacho* is a cold tomato soup. *Tapas* are small snacks, originating in southern Spain.

Pakistan and Bangladesh

- **Pakistan:** Capital: Islamabad. Population: 156.01 million. Currency: Pakistan rupee. Language: Urdu.
- **Bangladesh:** Capital: Dhaka. Population: 128.3 million. Currency: taka. Language: Bengali.
- **The Punjab** region is where many Pakistanis live. It gets its name—which means "five waters"—from five tributaries of the River Indus: the Jhelum, Chenab, Ravi, Sutlej, and Beus. These rivers water the Punjab's plains and make it fertile. All the same, large areas of the Punjab are dry and rely on one of the world's biggest irrigation networks.
- **Pakistan's major exports** include textiles, cement, leather, and machine tools.

▶ *Pakistan and Bangladesh were once one nation, East and West Pakistan, but East Pakistan broke away in 1971 to become Bangladesh.*

- **Buses, trucks, and rickshaws** in Pakistan are decorated with colorful patterns, pictures of movie stars, and religious themes. Many people think that the better the vehicle looks, the more careful the driver will be.
- **Pakistan's capital** is the city of Islamabad, built in the 1960s, but its biggest city and industrial center is the port of Karachi.
- **While people in India** are mainly Hindu, in Pakistan and Bangladesh they are mainly Muslim.
- **Jute is a reed** that thrives in Bangladesh's warm, moist climate. It is used for making rope, sacking, and carpet backing.
- **Over 70 big jute mills** make jute Bangladesh's most important export.
- **Most of Bangladesh** is low-lying and prone to flooding. Floods have devastated Bangladesh several times in the past 50 years.

Switzerland and Austria

- **Switzerland:** Capital: Berne. Population: 7.41 million. Currency: franc. Languages: German, French, and Italian.
- **Austria:** Capital: Vienna. Population: 8.1 million. Currency: euro. Language: German.
- **Switzerland and Austria** are small but beautiful countries mostly in the Alps mountains.
- **Both Switzerland and Austria** make a great deal of money from tourists who come to walk and ski here.
- **Switzerland** has long been "neutral," staying out of all the major wars. This is why organizations like the Red Cross and World Health Organization are based there.
- **Switzerland is** the second richest country in terms of GDP per person ($38,680). Luxembourg's is $45,320.
- **People from** all over the world put their money in Swiss banks because the country is stable politically and its banking laws guarantee secrecy.
- **Switzerland is famous** for making small, valuable things such as precision instruments and watches.
- **Vienna** was once the heart of the great Austrian Empire and the music capital of Europe.
- **Austrians** rely on mountain-river hydroelectricity for much of its power.

◀ *Austria earns more than a sixth of its income from tourists who come to enjoy the Alpine scenery.*

New England

▲ *New England is famous for the stunning colors of its trees in the fall, when the leaves turn to reds, golds, and ambers.*

- **New England** is six states in northeast U.S.A.—Maine, Vermont, New Hampshire, Massachusetts, Rhode Island, and Connecticut.
- **New England** was one of the first areas of North America settled by Europeans in the 1600s.
- **The U.S.A.'s** oldest buildings are in New England.
- **New England** is famous for its attractive small towns with pretty 18th- and 19th-century white clapboard houses and elegantly spired churches.
- **Vermont's** name means "green mountain" and it has fewer urban inhabitants than any other state.
- **Basketball** was invented in Massachusetts in 1891.
- **Route 128** in Massachusetts is famed for its cutting-edge electronic technology factories.
- **Boston** is one of the U.S.A.'s oldest, most cultured cities. It also has a large number of educational and research institutes. Harvard University is at Cambridge nearby. Yale is in Connecticut.
- **New Hampshire** is famous for its scenery.

★ STAR FACT ★

Rhode Island is the smallest state in the U.S.A., which is why it is often called "Little Rhody."

INDEX

I

J

K

L

M

N

O

P

ACKNOWLEDGMENTS

Artists: The publishers thank the following sources for the use of their photographs:
Page 8 (T/L) Wolfgang Kaehler/CORBIS; Page 8 (B/L) Patrick Johns/CORBIS; Page 11 (B/L) Wolfgang Kaehler/CORBIS; Page 14 (B/C) Paul A. Souders/CORBIS; Page 16 (T/C) Guy Stubbs, Gallo Images/CORBIS; Page 21 (B/R) Panos Pictures; Page 26 (B/L) Catherine Karnow/CORBIS; Page 33 (T/R) Ted Atkinson, Eye Ubiquitous/CORBIS; Page 39 (B/L) John Batholomew/CORBIS; Page 40 (B/L) Panos Pictures; Page 41 (B/R) Guy Stubbs, Gallo Images/CORBIS; Page 44 (T/L) David Cumming, Eye Ubiquitous/CORBIS; Page 47 (B/C) Jeffrey L. Rotman/CORBIS; Page 49 (C/L) Daewoo Cars Ltd.; Page 50 (B/L) Owen Franken/CORBIS; Page 51 (T/R) London Aerial Photo Library/CORBIS; Page 53 (B/R) Fancoise de Mulder/CORBIS; Page 54 (T/L) Kelly-Mooney Photography/CORBIS; Page 56 (B/L) Charles & Josette Lenars/CORBIS.
All other photographs are from MKP Archive.